Anonymous

Compilation of the Laws of Louisiana Relating to the Free

Public Schools

Vol. 3

Anonymous

Compilation of the Laws of Louisiana Relating to the Free Public Schools
Vol. 3

ISBN/EAN: 9783337779474

Printed in Europe, USA, Canada, Australia, Japan

Cover: Foto ©Suzi / pixelio.de

More available books at **www.hansebooks.com**

COMPILATION

OF THE

LAWS OF LOUISIANA

RELATING TO THE

FREE PUBLIC SCHOOLS,

EMBRACING ALL LAWS NOW IN FORCE,

FOR THE

PROPER MANAGEMENT AND GOVERNMENT
OF THE PUBLIC SCHOOLS.

ALSO OF THE

LAWS RELATING TO THE REVENUES FOR THE PUBLIC SCHOOLS,

AND A

DIGEST OF APPLYING DECISIONS

IS INCLUDED,

ALSO THE RULES AND REGULATIONS ADOPTED BY
THE STATE BOARD OF EDUCATION, ON THE
16TH DAY OF AUGUST, 1888.

ALSO A COMPLETE INDEX.

PREPARED IN COMPLIANCE WITH RESOLUTION OF THE STATE
BOARD OF EDUCATION.

———

" *The Government of the Child Should be Kingly.*" — ARISTOTLE.

———

NEW ORLEANS:
E. MARCHAND, STATE PRINTER, 110 CHARTRES ST.

———

1890.

PREFACE.

The favorable reception accorded the first edition of this compilation has induced the compiler to prepare a second, in which will be found all the matter embraced in the first substantially unchanged. New matter has been added, and the pamphlet in its present form will be found to contain information of practical value, not only to members of the different school boards, but as well to teachers and the patrons of the public schools generally.

While the compilation presents only such laws as the compiler finds in the Statutes relating to public education, and decisions of courts of high authority — also, the rules and regulations adopted by the State Board of Education, and an outline of studies, prepared, only as suggestions — he ventures to hope and believe that the compilation will prove useful, and assist in disseminating a more thorough knowledge of the school laws, and that the views expressed will coincide, in the main, with such as are held on the subject by worthy teachers, and by the friends and promoters of public education.   J. A. B.

March 1st, 1890.

THE TAXATION BY POLICE JURIES.

Is no longer limited. The local authorities having power to levy taxes, can increase the Parish taxation for schools. Several Parishes have increased the taxation above the maximum heretofore established under the repealed law.

COMFORT OF PUPILS.

The school boards have the authority to assess and collect one dollar per annum, to provide fuel, and for defraying the expenses necessary for the comfort of the pupils. Whenever possible, this amount should be collected and expended in the manner proposed.

SCHOOL HOUSES.

It is of the utmost importance to build school houses. The schools will be more permanent if inviting school houses be constructed. The law, authorizing the tax payers to tax themselves to construct improvements, has been copied in this compilation. It is explicit enough, and it affords a good opportunity to equably divide the expense of building school houses in the community. All of its members are equally interested in the management of excellent schools.

THE OFFICERS.

Under the present law, the duties of the officers are clearly defined. The school boards are entrusted with the important functions. The effectiveness of the school system depends in great part upon their exertion in behalf of the schools.

The Parish Superintendent is the secretary of the board, and executive officer. As the executive officer, he has the supervision of the different schools in charge. He should report their condition to the board, and see to the enforcement of the law, and to a thorough compliance, on the part of the teacher, with the duties devolved upon him. The faithful teacher has considerable to perform. His influence is far-reaching when his duties are attended with well directed energy. The community at once feels the importance of his services. The law in turn gives him authority over the pupils, to maintain proper discipline. Decisions are reported in this compilation on that subject.

With good judgment and care, and considerate intelligent action on his part, well regulated schools will prove highly useful and be maintained.

INSTITUTE OR TEACHER'S ASSOCIATION.

One of the features of the law adopted during the session of the General Assembly in 1888, relates to Parish Institutes. They are organized under the direction of the Parish Superintendent, and conducted by managing teacher. The law is not monitory. The Parish Superintendent may organize these Institutes. Whenever it is possible to organize a local Institute, it should not be neglected. It creates an interest in the cause of education that will result in a better and more cheerful support of the schools, and in an improvement in the teachers. It unites them, creates a healthier sympathy, and organizes a teacher force that must result in general improvement.

HYGIENE AND SCIENTIFIC TEMPERANCE.

A law has been adopted relative to hygiene; also with reference to the effects of narcotics, and requiring lessons to be taught on the subject on scientific temperance in all the schools. This requirement is important. It should be gradually introduced and taught in schools. More can be obtained by mild but firm teaching than arbitrary action.

THE LAW IN RELATION TO FREE SCHOOLS

The laws, the compilation of which is now presented to all those feeling an interest in the free schools, have been adopted after due deliberation. The best enaction will be as naught, if not enforced with some energy.

Energy and intelligent interest in behalf of the free schools, will bring about good results in a very short time.

The free school system has been made the cherished policy of the State and of the general government. It devolves upon the citizens to assist in developing that policy, and to aid in maintaining useful system of public education.

Jos. A. Breaux.

" The Hope of the World Lies in the Children."

There are many obligations of a public character imposed upon the citizens. They must serve as members of Juries; they may be called upon to bear arms to assert their country's rights; to serve in case of necessity in suppressing riots and insurrections, and in maintaining peace and order. This is not the limit of the functions of good citizenship. There are other important duties that should not be neglected. The influence of a man of liberal scholarship is considerable. The larger the number of citizens who have received training and culture the greater will be the influence for good, providing they choose to exercise for good, the advantages of education of which they have availed themselves. Every man is an agent of a great Almighty will. The greater the authority conferred upon him, the more general the procuration, the greater the responsibility.

The more important the object, the greater the attention it should receive. The education of future generations is certainly worthy of great attention.

Lord Macauly in his speech delivered in the House of Commons, on the 18th of April, 1847, said : " The education of the " people is not only a means, but the best means of attaining " that which all allow to be a chief end of the government, and if " this be so, it passes my faculties to understand how any man " can gravely contend that government has nothing to do with " the education of the people. * * * * ' Educate the peo- " ple,' was the first admonition addressed by Penn to the colony " which he founded ; ' educate the people,' said Lord Baltimore ; " ' educate the people,' was the legacy of Washington to the na- " tion he saved ; ' educate the people,' was the unceasing exhor- " tation of Jefferson. I quote Jefferson with peculiar pleasure, " because, of all the eminent men that ever lived (Adam Smith " himself not excepted), Jefferson was the one who most abhorred " everything like meddling on the part of governments, yet, the " chief business of his later years was to establish a good system " of State education in Virginia ; and against such authorities as " this, what have you, who take the other side, to show? Can " you mention a single great Philosopher? A single man distin- " guished by his love for liberty, humanity and truth, who, from " the beginning of the world down to the time of this present " parliament, have held your doctrines. You can oppose unani- " mous voice of all, the voice of all the wise and good, of all ages " and of both hemispheres, nothing but clamor which was first " heard a few months ago, a clamor which you cannot join with-

" out kindling, not only all whose memory you propose to hold in
" reverence, but even your former selves."

This was addressed to a minority quite limited of the govern-
ing classes of England. The influence of this minority is no
longer felt, for even England amply provides for general education. The influence of a man of liberal scholarship and of sound
educational views prevail.

The same responsibility rests upon the same classes of this
country; upon those who owe the culture they enjoy to the kind
and generous ancestry; upon those who owe to the State and to
the public schools the first lessons, and the foundation of the
knowledge they possess, devolve the duty. They are debtors in
this respect to future generations.   J. A. B.

What, sir! feed a child's body and let his soul hunger; pamper his limbs and starve his faculties? What! plant the earth, cover a thousand hills with your droves of cattle, pursue the fish to their hiding places in the sea, and spread your wheat fields across the plains in order to supply the wants of that body which will soon be as cold and senseless as the poorest clod, and let the spiritual essence within you, with all its glorious capacities for improvement, languish and pine? What! build factories, turn in rivers upon the water-wheels, unchain the imprisoned spirits of steam to weave a garment for the body and leave the soul unadorned and naked? What! send out your vessels to the farthest ocean and make battle with the monsters of the deep in order to obtain means for lighting up your dwelling, and permit that vital spark which Deity has kindled to languish and go out.

EDWARD EVERETT.

LIMITATION OF LEGISLATIVE POWERS.

Art. 51. No money shall ever be taken from the public treasury, directly or indirectly, in aid of any church, sect or denomination of religion, or in aid of any priest, preacher, minister or teacher thereof, as such; and no preference shall ever be given to, nor any distinction made against any church, sect or creed of religion, or any form of religious faith or worship; nor shall any appropriations be made for charitable or benevolent purposes to any person or community; provided, this shall not apply to the State Asylums for the insane, and deaf, dumb and blind, and the charity hospitals and public charitable institutions conducted under State authority.

ARTICLES OF THE STATE CONSTITUTION HAVING REFERENCE TO PUBLIC EDUCATION.

PROPERTY USED FOR COLLEGE AND SCHOOLS ARE EXEMPT FROM TAXATION.

Art. 207. The following property shall be exempt from taxation, and no other, viz: All public property, places of religious worship or burial, all charitable institutions, all buildings and property used exclusively for colleges, or other school purposes, the real and personal estate of any public library and that of any other literary association, used by or connected with such library; all books and philosophical apparatus, and all paintings and statuary of any company or association kept in a public hall; provided, the property so exempted be not used or leased for purpose of private or corporate profit or income. There shall also be exempt from taxation household property to the value of five hundred dollars; there shall also be exempt from taxation and license for a period of twenty years from the adoption of the Constitution of 1879, the capital, machinery and other property employed in the manufacture of textile fabrics, leather, shoes, harness, saddlery, hats, flour, machinery, agricultural implements, manufacture of ice, fertilizers and chemicals, and furniture and other articles of wood, marble, or stone, soap, stationery, ink and paper, boat building and chocolate; provided, that not less than five hands are employed in any one factory.

Art. 208. The General Assembly shall levy an annual poll-tax for the maintainance of public schools, upon every male inhabitant in the State, over the age of twenty-one years, which shall never be less than one dollar, nor exceed one dollar and a half per capita, and the General Assembly shall pass laws to enforce payment of said tax. * * * * * * * *

ART. 224. There shall be free public schools established by the General Assembly throughout the State, for the education of all the children of the State between the ages of six and eighteen years; and the General Assembly shall provide for their establishment, maintainance and support, by taxation or otherwise, and all moneys so raised, except the poll tax, shall be distributed to each parish in proportion to the number of children between the ages of six and eighteen years.

ART. 225 There shall be elected by the qualified voters of the State, a Superintendent of Public Education, who shall hold his office for the term of four years, and until his successor is qualified. His duties shall be prescribed by law, and he shall receive an annual salary of two thousand dollars.

The aggregate annual expenses of his office, including his salary, shall not exceed the sum of three thousand dollars. The General Assembly shall provide for the appointment of parish boards of public education for the different parishes.

The parish boards may appoint a parish superintendent of public schools in their respective parishes, who shall be ex-officio secretary of the parish board, and whose salary for his double functions shall not exceed two hundred dollars annually, except that in the parish of Orleans the salary of the parish superintendent shall be fixed by the General Assembly, to be paid out of the public school funds according to each parish respectively.

[One school board may sue another for recovery of funds illegally paid to the other. School Board of East Carroll vs. School Board of Union, 36 Ann. 806].

ART. 226. The general exercises in the public schools shall be conducted in the English language, and the elementary branches taught therein; provided, that these elementary branches may be also taught in the French language in those parishes in the State, or localities in said parish, where the French language predominates, it no additional expense is incurred thereby.

ART. 227. The funds derived from the collection of the poll-tax shall be applied exclusively to the maintenance of the public schools as organized under this constitution, and shall be applied exclusively to the support of the public schools in the parish in which the same shall be collected, and shall be accounted for and paid by the collecting officers directly to the competent school authorities of each parish.

ART. 228. No funds raised for the support of the public schools shall be appropriated for or used for the support of any other sectarian schools.

ART. 229. The school funds of this State shall consist of:

1. The proceeds of taxation for school purposes, as provided in the constitution.

2. The interest on the proceeds of all public lands heretofore granted by the United States for the use and support of the public schools.

3. Of all lands and other property which may hereafter be bequeathed, granted or donated to the State, or generally for school purposes.

4. All funds or property, other than unimproved lands, bequeathed or granted to the State, not designated for other purposes.

5. The proceeds of vacant estates falling under the law to the State of Louisiana.

The legislature may appropriate to the same fund the proceeds, in whole or in part, of public lands not designated for any other purposes, and shall provide that every parish may levy a tax for the public schools therein, which shall not exceed the State tax; provided, that with such tax the whole amount of parish taxes shall not exceed the limits of parish taxation fixed by this constitution.

CONCERNING A STATE UNIVERSITY.

ART. 230. The University of Louisiana, as at present established and located at New Orleans, is hereby recognized in its three departments—to-wit: the law, the medical and the agricultural departments—to be governed and controlled by appropriate faculties. The General Assembly shall, from time to time, make such provision for the proper government, maintenance and support of said State University of Louisiana, and all the departments thereof, as the public necessity and well-being of the people of the State of Louisiana may require, not to exceed ten thousand dollars annually.

The Louisiana State University and Agricultural and Mechanical College, now established and located in the city of Baton Rouge, is hereby recognized, and all revenues derived and to be derived from the sales of land or land scrip, donated by the United States to the State of Louisiana for the use of seminary of learning, and mechanical and agricultural college, shall be appropriated exclusively to the maintenance and support of said University and Mechanical and Agricultural College, and the General Assembly shall from time to time make such additional appropriations for the maintenance and support of said Louisiana State University and Agricultural and Mechanical College as the public necessities and the well-being of the people of the State of Louisiana may require, not to exceed ten thousand dollars annually.

(See Act 43, of 1884, Tulane Amendment).

ART. 231. The General Assembly shall also establish in the city of New Orleans a University for the education of persons of color, provide for its proper government, and shall make an annual appropriation of not less than five thousand dollars, nor more than ten thousand dollars for its maintenance and support.

Warrants for salaries of constitutional officers where amounts are fixed by constitution, are paid by preference and property over all warrants on General Fund. State ex rel Collins vs. Burke, 32 Ann. 1250; State ex rel University vs. Burke, 35 Ann. 404.

University warrants issued of these articles have priority over all others, except constitutional warrants. State ex rel University of Louisiana vs. Burke, 35 Ann. 457.

After payment of University and Constitutional warrants, the Legislature may regulate priority of payment of other warrants. But where general fund cannot meet all apportions after payment of these two classes, and those having legislative priority, such appropriations share the residue pro rata. (State ex rel Bier vs. Burke, 37 Ann. 434).

ART. 232. Women over twenty-one years of age shall be eligible to any office of control or management under the school laws of this State.

THE FREE SCHOOL FUND, SEMINARY FUND, AND AGRICULTURAL AND MECHANICAL FUND.

ART. 233. The debt due by the State to the free school fund is hereby declared to be the sum of one million, one hundred and thirty thousand, eight hundred and sixty-seven 51-100 dollars in principal, and shall be placed on the books of the Auditor to the credit of the several townships entitled to the same; the said principle being the proceeds of the sales of land heretofore granted by the United States for the use and support of free public schools, which amount shall be held by the State as a loan, and shall be and remain a perpetual fund, on which the State shall pay an annual interest of four per cent, from the first day of January, 1880, and that said interest shall be paid on the several townships in the State, entitled to the same in accordance with the act of Congress, No. 68, approved February 5, 1843; and the bonds of the State heretofore issued belonging to said fund, and sold under the act of the General Assembly, No. 81, of 1872, are hereby declared null and void, and the General Assembly shall make no provision for their payment, and may cause them to be destroyed.

The debt due by the State to the Seminary fund is hereby declared to be one hundred and thirty-six thousand dollars, being the proceeds of the sales of the land heretofore granted by the United States to the State, for the use of a Seminary of Learning, and said amount shall be placed to the credit of said fund on the books of the Auditor of the State, as a perpetual loan, and the State shall pay an annual interest of four per cent on said amount from January 1st, 1880, for the use of said Seminary of Learning; and the consolidated bonds of the State now held for the use of said fund shall be null and void after the first day of January, 1880, and the General Assembly shall never make any provision for their payment, and they shall be destsoyed in such manner as the General Assembly may direct.

The debt due by the State to the Agricultural and Mechanical College fund is hereby declared to be the sum of one hundred and eighty-two thousand, three hundred and thirteen $\frac{3}{100}$ dollars, being the proceeds of the sales of lands and land scrip heretofore granted by the United States to this State, for the use of a College for the benefit of agriculture and mechanic arts; said amounts shall be placed to the credit of said fund on the books of the Auditor and Treasurer of the State, as a perpetual loan, and the State shall pay an annual interest of five per cent on said amount from January 1st, 1880, for the use of said Agricultural and Mechanical College. The consolidated bonds of the State now held by the State for the use of said fund, shall be null and void after the first day of January, 1880, and the General Assembly shall not make any provision for their payment, and they shall be destroyed in such manner as the General Assembly may direct.

The interest provided for by this article shall be paid out of any tax that may be levied and collected for the general purposes of public education.

The teacher is a power. Leaving out of view their hereditary bias and their home environments, pupils become in a large measure what the teachers make them. Like teacher, like pupil. The teacher cannot be successful unless he becomes in some way a dominating influence in his pupil's life. He must be the ever present help, not only when with the child, but away from him, acting as a tonic to his mental energy, and furnishing motives for his self-sacrifices, and touching the sky of his future life and hope.

J. H. MATTHEWS.

GENERAL ACT.

No. 81] ADOPTED SESSION OF 1888.

[See Act 43 of 1884, Tulane Amendment.]

To regulate public education in Louisiana; to provide a revenue for the same, and impose certain penalties; and to apply fines imposed by District Courts, and amounts collected on bonds to the purpose of public education, and to provide for the payment of unpaid balances due the public school teachers of New Orleans, for the years 1880, 1881, 1882 and 1884.

ARTICLE I.—STATE BOARD OF EDUCATION.

SECTION 1. That the Governor and the Superintendent of Public Education, and the Attorney General, together with six citizens to be appointed by the Governor, one from each Congressional District of the State, shall be a body politic and corporate by the name and style of the Board of Education for the State of Louisiana, with authority to sue and defend suits in all matters relating to the interest of the public schools. The above specified six citizens shall receive, as compensation for their services in attending the meetings of the board, their actual traveling expenses and *per diem* for the number of days that the board is in session, the same as members of the State Legislature, payable on their warrants, approved by the president and secretary of the board, out of the school fund.

ART. II.—AUTHORITY AND DUTY OF THE STATE BOARD OF EDUCATION.

SEC. 2. That the Governor shall be *ex-officio* the president, and the State Superintendent the secretary. The board shall meet on or before the first Monday of December of each year, and at other times upon the call of the State Superintendent. The acts of the board shall be attested by the signature of the president.

ART. III.—PAROCHIAL BOARDS OF SCHOOL DIRECTORS, RULES FOR THE GOVERNMENT OF SCHOOLS AND UNIFORMITY OF TEXT BOOKS.

SEC. 3. That the State Board of Education shall appoint for each parish in the State, except the parish of Orleans, a board of school directors consisting of not less than five, nor more than nine, qualified citizens of the parish. The Governor shall issue a commission to each of said directors. The State Board of Education shall prepare rules, by-laws and regulations for the government of the common schools of the State, which shall be enforced by the parish superintendents and the several school boards, and shall give such directions as it may see proper as to the branches of study which shall be taught. The State Board shall strictly enforce a uniformity of text books in all the public schools, and shall adopt a list thereof, which shall remain unchanged for four years after such adoption. For satisfactory reasons shown to said board, it may change said list or adopt a list generally preferred by teachers or parents in certain localities, maintaining as far as possible a uniformity of text books, and without placing parents and guardians to further expense. The adoption of such list and aparatus shall be by contract to the lowest bidder, subject to the change aforesaid, and to the best advantage as to cost to pupils.

ART. IV.—PARISH SUPERINTENDENT; ADDITIONAL REPORT MAY BE REQUIRED OF HIM BY THE STATE BOARD OF EDUCATION.

SEC. 4. That the State Board of Education may require reports to be made by the parish superintendent whenever the interest of the common schools indicate the necessity of other reports than now required.

ART. V.—TERM OF OFFICE OF THE MEMBERS OF THE PARISH BOARDS AND OF THE PARISH SUPERINTENDENTS.

SEC. 5. That the term of office of the members of the parish school boards and of the parish superintendents shall be four years from the time of their appointment. If a vacancy occurs, the unexpired term shall be filled as hereinbefore provided. These officers shall take the usual oath of office, which oath shall be filed in the office of the State Superintendent of Public Education.

ART. VI.—SCHOOL BOARDS ARE BODIES CORPORATE.

SEC. 6. That the several school boards are constituted bodies corporate, with power to sue and be sued, under the name and style of the "Parish Board of Directors of the Parish of——," as the case may be. Citations shall be served on the president of the board.

ART. VII.—DUTY AND AUTHORITY OF PARISH BOARDS.

SEC. 7.—That the parish board of directors shall select from their number a president. They shall elect or appoint a parish superintendent, who shall be ex-officio secretary of the board. They are authorized, in their discretion, to appoint auxiliary visiting trustees for each ward or school district, or school in the parish; such trustees to make quarterly reports to the parish boards of the actual condition of, and shall make needful suggestions in all matters relating to the schools they have in charge as trustee.

The parish board of directors shall report to the State Board of Education all deficiencies in the schools, or neglect of duty on the part of teachers, superintendent or other officer. They shall visit and examine the schools in the several school districts of the parish, from time to time, and they shall meet and advise with the trustees when occasion requires (if auxiliary trustees be appointed by the board of the parish) They shall apportion the school fund to the several districts in the parish in proportion to the number of persons in the district between the ages of six and eighteen years, and shall determine the number of schools to be opened, the location of the school houses, the number of teachers to be employed, their salary; and the said school board is entrusted with seeing that the provisions of the law are complied with. They shall make such rules and by-laws for their own government (not inconsistent with the law) as they may deem proper. The regular meeting of each parish board shall be held on the first Saturday of January, April, July and October, and it may hold such special and adjourned meetings as the board may determine, or as occasion may require. Each member shall receive payment for his attendance at school board meetings, when the board shall hold regular sessions on the days before mentioned; provided, that the amount be not fixed by the said board at more than two dollars per diem, and provided that the whole amount expended annually shall not exceed one hundred dollars. The school boards shall exercise proper vigilance in securing for the schools of the parish all funds destined for the support of the schools, including the State fund apportioned thereto, the poll tax collectible, and all other funds. They shall keep a record of all their transactions and proceedings. The school boards may receive land by purchase or donation, for the purpose of erecting a school house, provide for and secure the erection of same, construct such outbuildings and enclosures as shall be conductive to the protection of the property, make repairs and provide the necessary furniture and apparatus. All contracts for improvements shall be to the lowest responsible bidder, the board reserving the right to reject any and all bids. They shall have power to recover for any damages that may be done the property in their charge; they may, by a two third vote of the whole board, after due notice, change the location of the school-house, sell or dispose of the old site and use the proceeds thereof towards procuring a new one.

ART. VIII.—REMOVAL OF PARISH SUPERINTENDENTS, AND

THEIR APPEALS.

SEC. 8. For sufficient cause, the parish board of school directors may remove the parish superintendent, subject to an appeal to the State Board of Education, provided this appeal be taken within ten days after his dismissal. The appeal shall not have the effect of suspending the board's action of dismissal during its pendency, but the parish superintendent shall be reinstated if the State Board of Education décides that he was dismissed without cause, and reverses the decision of the parish school board.

ART. IX.—ATTORNEY OF THE PARISH BOARDS.

SEC. 9. That the district attorney of the district, or any other attorney selected by the board, shall act as counsel for the parish board.

ART. X.—GRADED AND HIGH SCHOOLS AND AUTHORITY OF THE PAROCHIAL BOARDS IN THAT CONNECTION.

SEC. 10. That the parish school board shall have the authority to establish graded schools, and to adopt such a system in that connection as may be necessary to assure their success; central or high schools may be established when necessary. The ordinances establishing such schools adopted by the parish school boards shall be submitted to the State Board of Education, and no high school shall be opened without its sanction, and no such school shall be established unless the amount be donated for the site and suitable buildings are provided for without any expense out of the school fund; provided, that the boards of directors of the parish of Orleans shall not require the sanction of the State Board for the purposes aforesaid. The school boards shall have the authority to assess and collect one dollar per annum from each family, surviving parent or guardian, who actually sends a child or children to the common schools of the district, to be collected in such manner as said board shall determine, which amount shall be used in providing the school-house with fuel and defraying the expenses necessary for the comfort of the school.

ART. XI.—DIVISION OF PARISHES INTO SCHOOL DISTRICTS.

SEC. 11. That it shall be the duty of the parish board with the parish superintendent to divide the parish into school districts of such proper and convenient area and shape as will best accommodate the children of the parish. The parish boards shall, as soon as practicable, proceed to the work imposed upon them, and upon completing this work, they shall make a report to the parish superintendent, which report shall contain the boundary and description of the said district designated by number. The parish superintendent shall record the same in a well bound book, kept by him for the purpose, which book shall be held by said parish superintendent, and be at all times open to inspection. The parish board, if they deem it to the best interests of the schools, may divide the parish into districts without reference to the wards in the parish.

ART. XII.—SCHOOL DISTRICTS IN TWO ADJOINING PARISHES—
HOW LAID OFF.

SEC. 12. That the parish superintendents of two adjoining parishes, where the division line intersects a neighborhood whose convenience requires it, may lay off a district composed of parts of both the parishes. Such districts shall be reported, together with the census of school children only as belonging to the parish in which the school house may be situated, by the parish superintendent of the parish; and report shall be made by the assessor and the parish superintendent as though it lay entirely in the parish.

ART. XIII.—OPTION WHEN SCHOOL DISTRICTS ADJOIN AS TO
WHICH SCHOOL CERTAIN CHILDREN WILL ATTEND.

SEC. 13. That, where two school districts adjoin, it shall be lawful for the children in either of the said adjoining districts to be taught in and at such school-house as shall be most convenient to them; provided, that their tuition fees shall be paid to the district in which they are taught, and that no change be made without the assent of the school boards of the respective parishes.

ART. XIV.—BRANCHES TO BE TAUGHT, ALSO THE FRENCH LAN-
GUAGE IN THOSE LOCALITIES WHERE THE FRENCH
LANGUAGE PREDOMINATES

SEC. 14.—That the branches of orthography, reading, writing, arithmetic, geography, grammar, United States history and laws of health shall be taught in every district. In addition to those, such other branches as the State Board of Education and the parish school board may require; provided. that these elementary branches may be also taught in the French language in those parishes in the State or localities in said parishes where the French language predominates, if no additional expense is incurred.

ART. XV.—DUTIES OF THE PRESIDENT OF THE SCHOOL BOARD.

SEC. 15. That the president shall preside at the meetings of the board, call special meetings when necessary, advise with and assist the parish superintendent in promoting the success of the schools, and generally do and perform all other acts and duties pertaining to his office of president of the board. All deeds and contracts for the schools, including those with teachers, are to be signed by him; the latter also by the parish superintendent.

SECRETARY — HIS DUTIES.

The secretary shall keep full minutes of all proceedings of the board in a book provided for the purpose, and shall do and perform all other acts and duties legally pertaining to the office of secretary of the board.

ART. XVI.—STATE SUPERINTENDENT OF PUBLIC EDUCATION.

SEC. 16. That an office shall be provided for the State Superintendent of Public Education at the seat of government, in which he shall file, each year separately, all papers, reports and public documents transmitted to him by the board and officers whose duty it is to report to him, and hold the same in readiness to be examined by the Governor whenever he sees proper, and by any committee appointed by the General Assembly; and he shall cause to be kept a record of all matters appertaining to his office. In case of vacancy in the office of Superintendent of Public Education, the Governor shall fill the vacancy and submit the name of the appointee to the Senate for its confirmation at the first session held after the appointment.

ART. XVII —SALARY OF THE STATE SUPERINTENDENT, HIS OFFICE, STATIONERY, CLERK, PORTER.

SEC. 17. That the salary of the Superintendent of Public Education shall be two thousand dollars per annum, besides which he shall be entitled to office fixtures, stationery, books, fuel and lights needed to carry on the work of his office. He shall have the authority to appoint a clerk and a porter, and prescribe the duties of each; provided, that the entire expenses of his office, including salaries, postage and incidentals, shall not exceed the specific appropriation therefor, payable in monthly installments out of the current school fund by the Treasurer of the State, upon the warrants of the State Superintendent.

ART. XVIII.—DUTIES OF THE STATE SUPERINTENDENT AND THE SCHOOLS SUBJECT TO HIS SUPERVISORY CONTROL.

SEC. 18. That the State Superintendent of Public Education shall have general supervision of all boards of education and of all common, high and normal schools of the State, and shall see that the school system is carried into effect properly. He shall visit the several parishes of the State whenever practicable, at least once a year, and shall give due notice of the time of his intended visit to the parish superintendent, whose duty it shall be to meet and confer with the State Superintendent on all matters connected with the interests of the common schools of the parish; while engaged in this duty his actual expenses shall be paid out of the current school fund, but shall not in any case exceed the amount appropriated per annum for the purpose.

ART. XIX.—ACCOUNTS THE STATE SUPERINTENDENT SHALL KEEP.

SEC. 19. That he shall keep an account of all orders drawn or countersigned by him on the Auditor of all returns of settlements, and make note of all changes in the appointment of school treasurers; whenever required any part of this account or note of change shall be furnished by the Auditor.

ART. XX.—BIENNIAL REPORT AND WHAT IT SHALL CONTAIN,
AND NUMBER OF COPIES TO BE PRINTED
AND DISTRIBUTED.

SEC. 20. That he shall biennially, on or before the meeting of the General Assembly, make a report of the condition and progress made and possible improvements to be made in the common schools; the amount and condition of the school funds; how its revenues, during two previous school years, have been distributed; the amount collected and disbursed for common school purposes from local taxation or from any other source of revenue, and how the same was expended.

This report shall contain an abstract of the parish and city superintendents' reports. He shall communicate all facts, statistics and information as are of interest to the common schools. He shall cause to be printed a copy for each school district in the State, two hundred copies for the use of the members of the Legislature and to exchange with the superintendents of public instruction of other States, and three hundred copies for distribution by the superintendent.

ART. XXI.—INSTITUTION OF THE BLIND AND THE DEAF AND
DUMB. REPORTS AND SUGGESTIONS TO BE MADE
BY THE STATE SUPERINTENDENT.

SEC. 21. That the Superintendent in his report shall set forth the objects, make suggestions which may be of interest and promote the success of the Institutions of the Blind and the Deaf and Dumb. The superintendents of these institutions shall annually, by the first day of March, furnish the State Superintendent of Public Education such statements of their respective institutions as may be necessary to enable him to make a full and satisfactory report.

ART. XXII.—COPIES OF THE STATE SUPERINTENDENT'S RECORDS
AND PAPERS ADMISSIBLE IN EVIDENCE.

SEC. 22. That certified copies of records and papers in his office shall, in all cases, be evidence as admissible as the original.

ART. XXIII —NEGLECT OF DUTY TO BE REPORTED AND THE
IMPROPER USE OF THE SCHOOL FUND.

SEC. 23. That it is made part of his duty to report all neglect of duty or any improper uses made of school funds to the State Board of Education whenever it may come to his knowledge.

ART. XXIV.—DECISIONS TO BE MADE BY THE STATE SUPERIN-
TENDENT AND APPEALS FROM HIS DECISIONS.

SEC. 24. That the State Superintendent shall decide all controversies or disputes that may arise or exist among the directors, or between the superintendents and the board, and between the superintendents and teachers concerning their respective duties. The facts of these controversies or disputes shall be made known to him by written statements by the parties thereto, verified by oath or affirmation if required, and accompanied by certified copies of all necessary minutes, contracts, orders or other documents. An appeal may be taken from his decision to the Board of Education, provided it be taken within fifteen days after his decision shall have been made. When called upon by the Superintendent of Public Education the Attorney General shall give his opinion in regard to any controversy or dispute. The Superintendent of Public Education shall, whenever required, give advice, explanations, constructions or informations to the district officers and superintendents and citizens relative to the common school law; the duties of common school officers; the right and duties of parents, guardians, pupils and all officers; the management of the schools, and all other questions calculated to promote the cause of education.

ART. XXV.—PARISH SUPERINTENDENT.

SEC. 25. That there shall be a parish superintendent in each of the parishes of the State, the parish of Orleans excepted, who shall be possessed of moral character and ability to manage the common school interest of the parish. He shall be of age. His salary shall not be more than two hundred dollars per annum for his services as superintendent and secretary as herei provided.

ART. XXVI.—VISITS TO BE MADE.

SEC. 26. That he shall during the year visit, once at least, each district school in the parish, and he shall exert his best endeavors in promoting the cause of common school education.

ART. XXVII.—ADDITIONAL COMPENSATION ALLOWED FOR CERTAIN SERVICES OF THE PARISH SUPERINTENDENT.

SEC. 27 Whenever his services are quite efficient and highly satisfactory to the school board, it is authorized in its discretion to allow an amount sufficient to the parish superintendent to defray his expenses in visiting all the schools in his parish. The amount allowed shall never exceed one hundred and twenty five dollars per annum. Prior to any payment for expenses in visiting the schools he shall make a written report respecting the condition of each school examined, and shall make it appear that he has devoted at least three hours in examining each school visited. The school board is also authorized to defray his expenses to attend annually the convention of superintendents.

ART. XXVIII.—COMMITTEE FOR THE SELECTION OF TEACHERS.

SEC. 28. That the president of the school board and a member appointed by the board, also the Parish Superintendent, shall constitute a committee, and shall as such appoint the teachers of the common schools for his parish, and fill vacancies in the order of merit as hereinafter provided. At the first meeting of the board after the appointment, it shall be noted in each instance in the minutes of its proceedings.

ART. XXIX.—REPORT OF SCHOOL CHILDREN IN EACH PARISH AND DISTRICT, WHEN TO BE MADE AND BY WHOM.

SEC. 29. That it shall be the duty of each Parish Superintendent, on or before the 10th day of January of each year, to cause to be placed in the hands of the State Superintendent of Public Education a report showing the number of children between the ages of six and eighteen years, residing in the parish, and the whole number residing in each district designated by this number. He shall take the items of his report from the assessor's returns showing the said number of children, but he shall assure himself of its correctness, and so attest before a competent officer.

ART. XXX.—REPORT ANNUALLY BY THE PARISH SUPERIN-
TENDENT, TO WHOM MADE, WHEN, WHAT IT SHALL CONTAIN,
AND PENALTY FOR FAILURE TO MAKE THE REPORT.

SEC. 30. That he shall previously to the 15th day of January, mail to the State Superintendent of Public Education his official report, showing in tables an aggregate of the school districts in his parish by number, the districts in which schools were taught, and the length of time taught, the highest, the lowest, and the average number of children at school, the cost of tuition of each child for the session and per month, number of private schools, academies and colleges taught in the parish, and the length of session of same; the number of teachers employed, male and female, for the common schools, the average wages of male teachers, female teachers, the amount of money raised for school purposes in the parish by local tax or otherwise, and for whose purpose it was disbursed; the number and kind of school houses, and the value of each, the number built during the year preeceding the report, the number of district libraries and the number of volumes in each, and the increase during the year, the amount received and expended. In case of his neglect or failure to make this report in time as required, he shall forfeit and pay the sum of twenty dollars of his annual salary.

ART. XXXI.—RECORD THEY SHALL KEEP, DESCRIPTIONS OF SCHOOL DISTRICTS, CUSTODY OF PAPERS AND DOCUMENTS.

SEC. 31. That each Parish Superintendent shall keep a record of all the business transacted by him as Parish Superintendent, the names and numbers, and description of school districts, and all other papers and documents of value connected with his office, at all times subject to inspection and examination by any school officer or other person interested in any question pertaining to the common school.

ART. XXXII.---OATHS THEY MAY ADMINISTER.

Sec. 32. That the Parish Superintendent may administer the oath required of any of the officials of the common schools, or of any person required to make oath in any matter relating thereto, except to qualify directors

ART. XXXIII.----OFFICE DAYS OF THE PARISH SUPERINTENDENT.

Sec 33. That he shall attend at his office, at the parish seat, on the first Saturday of January, April, July and October, in each year, and at such other times as may be necessary for him to receive the reports of teachers and others, and to transact the business required of him.

ART. XXXIV.---TEACHERS' INSTITUTE OR ASSOCIATION.

Sec. 34. The Parish Superintendent may devote the first Saturday of each month, during the time the common schools are in session in the parish, to holding institutes for the improvement of teachers in their qualifications and methods of teaching, and for the discussion of topics pertaining to the advancement of the public school interest in the parish.

ART. XXXV.----ATTENDANCE OF THE TEACHERS' OBLIGATORY.

Sec. 35. That the teachers shall be notified of the time and place of the monthly institute meeting. Teachers failing to be present, or to take such part in the exercises as the Superintendent may assign or designate, shall forfeit one day's salary (which forfeited salary shall be paid to the parish institute fund), unless a good and sufficient reason for such failure to attend shall be given in writing to the parish Superintendent within ten days thereafter. No teacher shall be bound to attend the institute who, to do so, shall have to travel a greater distance than ten miles each way, and otherwise than by land.

ART. XXXVI.---LENGTH OF TIME FOR SESSIONS AND FORFEITURE FOR NON-ATTENDANCE.

Sec. 36. Three hours work shall be required to constitute a legal session of one institute, and the Parish Superintendent shall forfeit five dollars for each institute that he fails to conduct as required by this act, unless physically unable to attend, or for other sufficient excuse, to the satisfaction of the School Board.

ART. XXXVII—MEMBERS OF THESE INSTITUTES MAY BE HONORARY OR ACTIVE.

Sec. 37. These institutes may receive as members, honorary or active, the members of the board, all officers, and any citizen of good moral character as may desire to become a member, subject to the rules and regulations, and to the payment of such dues and fines as may be imposed by a quorum of the said institutes.

ART. XXXVIII.—ROLL OF MEMBERS.

SEC. 38. That each parish superintendent, upon the assembling of the teachers' institute of his parish, shall cause a roll of members to be prepared, which roll shall be called at least twice a day during the session of the institute, and all absentees shall be carefully marked. He shall ascertain the number of teachers who were in attendance, and length of time each attended, and he shall keep a record thereof.

ART. XXXIX.—INSTITUTE MANAGERS IN THE PARISHES.

SEC. 39. That each parish superintendent before the begining of the free school term, shall appoint one of the best qualified teachers of his parish as institute manager for each institute district, should there be more than one institute district in the parish; and such appointees shall each be paid for actual services two dollars and a half per day out of the institute fund as compensation for holding institutes, and for assisting the superintendent during the session.

ART. XL.—INSTITUTE FUND. HOW COLLECTED, KEPT AND EXPENDED.

SEC. 40. That all institute funds shall be collected and receipted for by the superintendent He shall have a record of the amount received, hand them over to the treasurer of the school board, who shall keep a separate account of these funds. He shall pay them out on the warrant of the superintendent, countersigned by the president of the school board. These funds shall be expended only in the interest of the institutes. The superintendent, for all services in connection with these institutes, shall be paid three dollars a day out of said fund for each day he will cause the said institute, to hold under his personal superintendence, and for each day's attendance as provided for in section thirty four (34).

ART. XLI.—INSTITUTE NOT APPLICABLE TO NEW ORLEANS.

SEC. 41. The foregoing sections having reference to parish institutes shall not apply to the parish of Orleans, but the school board of said parish may inaugurate and carry on such institutes in the manner and with the power and authority set forth above.

ART. XLII.—INSTITUTES ORDERED TO BE HELD BY THE STATE BOARD. ATTENDANCE AND HOW HELD.

SEC. 42. That other institutes may be held when ordered by the State board of education or under special laws ordering such institutes to be held. These shall be held at any time ordered by authority between the first day of April and the first day of October. Every teacher of a common school must attend the sessions upon penalty for non-attendance, and if satisfactory excuse has not been rendered to the parish superintendent of forfeiting two days' pay. Those sessions, i. e., those provided for by this section, shall not be held during a longer time than four days; during which there shall be vacation of the common schools of the parishes, to give opportunity to the teachers to attend, and no reduction of the teacher's salary shall be made during said vacation, provided he was in attendance the full time of the session of the institute. These institutes, held under this section, shall, as far as possible, be held in some town centrally located, and teachers from as many parishes as can conveniently attend shall be notified to attend. This notice they shall obey, under the penalty, if not obeyed, before mentioned. That at each session of the institute, every subject embraced in the common school cause shall be brought before the institute; also, shall be considered the whole work of the teacher, and the common school laws of the State shall be read and expounded.

ART. XLIII.—REPORTS TO BE MADE BY PARISH SUPERINTEN-
DENTS RESPECTING INSTITUTES.

SEC. 43. That the parish superintendent, in his annual report to the State superintendent, shall state the time and place teachers institutes were held; the names of the persons conducting the same; the number of persons registered as in attendance; the sums collected; the number and names of teachers of common schools in the parish who did not attend the institute, and such other information of the proceedings and results of the institute as he may deem of value and interest.

ART. XLIV.—EXAMINATION OF APPLICANTS TO BE APPOINTED
TEACHERS. BY WHOM CONDUCTED AND HOW.

SEC. 44. That it shall be the duty of the parish superintendent to conduct or superintend in person the examination of all persons offering themselves as candidates for position of teachers of the common schools of his parish (except in cities and towns organized as one district by special act of the General Assembly; except also, when the applicant holds a certificate entitling him to teach without further examination, as provided for in this act,) in regard to their moral character, learning and ability to teach. For any violation of this duty he shall be liable to a fine of not less than twenty dollars, nor more than fifty dollars. The school board of the parish shall appoint a committee of two competent persons to assist him (the parish superintendent) in making these examinations. The superintendent and the committee must agree as to competency of the applicant before a certificate can be issued. Whenever two or more teachers apply for the same position or positions a competitive examination shall be held, and the position or positions shall be given to the most competent.

ART. XLV.—EXAMINATION FEE.

SEC. 45. Before being examined, each applicant for a certificate to teach shall pay a fee of one dollar for the parish institute fund, which shall be returned to him if a certificate be not issued to him.

ART. XLVI.—EXAMINERS. THEIR DUTIES AND PENALTIES FOR NON-PERFORMANCE.

SEC. 46. Before the examiners shall commence their examination of teachers, they shall take an oath that they will faithfully discharge their duties; they shall not give to any person a certificate before they will have examined the candidate touching his or her qualifications and fitness to teach, and who is not qualified to teach as required by the common school law. They shall be satisfied that the applicant is possessed of good moral character; if at any time the teacher be found incompetent, inefficient or unworthy of the endorsement given him, the parish superintendent may revoke the same and notify the board of his action for its approval or disapproval. Any teacher may be discharged at any time under the above provisions, but he shall be entitled to receive payment for services only up to the time of such dismissal.

ART. XLVII.—THIRD GRADE CERTIFICATE.

SEC. 47. To obtain a third grade certificate the applicant must be found competent to teach spelling, reading, primary mental arithmetic, rudiments of practical arithmetic through fractions and simple interest, elementary geography, primary language lessons and laws of health.

ART. XLVIII—SECOND GRADE CERTIFICATE.

SEC. 48. To obtain a second grade certificate the applicant must be found competent to teach arithmetic, geography, English grammar and composition, United States history, elements of natural philosophy and elements of physiology.

ART. XLIX.—FIRST GRADE CERTIFICATE.

SEC. 49. To obtain a high school or first grade certificate the applicant must be found competent to teach elocution, spelling, grammar, rhetoric and literature, history, botany, philosophy, arithmetic, algebra, geography and geometry, and such other studies of high grade as local boards may deem necessary. A special certificate of this grade may issue on a satisfactory examination in the study or studies to be taught in any special academic department, which shall entitle the holder to special appointment in a department where such studies may be taught.

ART. L.—CERTIFICATE REQUIRED AS A REQUISITE TO THE EM-
PLOYMENT OF A TEACHER.

SEC. 50. That no person shall be appointed to teach who has
not obtained a license for the scholastic year in which the school
is to be taught, and of a grade sufficiently high to meet the requirements of the school, or unless he or she holds a certificate
provided for by this act, which exempts him or her from examination; provided, that all teachers who have been teaching
since three years are exempt from further examination.

ART. LI. —REGISTER AND REPORT TO BE MADE MONTHLY BY
TEACHERS.

SEC. 51. That it shall be the duty of each teacher of a common
school to keep such a register of the school as the parish superintendent may require, and prior to receiving his or her monthly
salary at the end of each month, he or she shall make a report of
the entire number of pupils enrolled; the highest, lowest and
average number of pupils in attendance during the session; the
books used, branches taught, number of pay pupils, if any, and
such other information as the parish superintendent may deem
important, and shall furnish a copy of such report to the parish
superintendent, and if he or she willfully neglect or fail to do
this the parish superintendent shall withhold two dollars ($2) of
his salary due for the benefit of the parish institute.

ART. LII.—STUDIES PRESCRIBED BY THE BOARD TO BE FOLLOWED
AND ACCOUNTABILITY OF PUPILS TO TEACHERS.

SEC. 52. That the teachers shall faithfully enforce in school
the course of study and the regulations prescribed in pursuance
of law, and if any teacher shall wilfully refuse or neglect to comply with such requisitions, the parish superintendent, on petition
or complaint which shall be deemed sufficient by the board, may
remove or dismiss him or her. Every teacher shall have the
power and authority to held every pupil to a strict accountability
in school for any disorderly conduct on the play grounds of the
school or during intermission or recess, and to suspend from
school any pupil for good cause; provided, however, that such
suspension shall be reported in writing as soon as practicable to
the parish superintendent, whose decision of the case shall be
final; and, provided further, that in the parish of Orleans the
principals of schools shall suspend and report same to the superintendent for approval or further action.

ART. LIII.—REVENUE

SEC. 53. That the State Superintendent of Public Education
shall quarterly, on the first Monday in March, June, September
and December, in each year, apportion the funds appropriated by
the General Assembly for the support of the common schools of
the State, among the several parishes of the State, according to

the number of children between the ages of six and eighteen years in each parish; provided, however, that all the poll tax collected in any parish shall be appropriated to said parish. The amount so apportioned shall be paid by the State Treasurer to the school treasurer of each parish upon the warrant of the State Superintendent of Public Education.

ART. LIV.---POLICE JURIES AND ALL MUNICIPAL CORPORATIONS EXCEPT NEW ORLEANS, TO LEVY 1½ MILLS FOR SCHOOL PURPOSES IN THEIR ANNUAL BUDGET.

SEC. 54. That the police jurors of the several parishes, and the boards of trustees, aldermen, and legal representatives of cities, towns and villages (except the parish of Orleans), may levy for the support of the common schools of their respective parishes, not less that one and a half mills of the ten mills tax on the dollar of the assessed valuation of the property thereof. This shall be provided for in their annual budgets. On the refusal or neglect to levy said tax or to vote for such levy, the parish school board shall have the right, and it shall be its duty, to compel by mandamus, which may be tried in chambers or in open court, the levy of said tax to be collected as in case of parish and coporation taxes, and shall be paid to the school treasury of the parish or town where collected, monthly, by the tax collector; prov ded, towns not exempted under their charters from the payment of parish taxes, and subjected to the burden of taxation as the parishes are, shall not pay this tax, for same is included in the taxes imposed by the parish in which the town is situated.

NOTA.—The Legislature may appropriate to same fund the proceeds, in whole or in part, of public lands not designated for any other purpose, and shall provide that every parish may levy a tax for the public schools therein, which shall not exceed the State tax; provided, that with such tax the whole amount of parish taxes shall not exceed the limits of parish taxation fixed by the Cons itution. Const. Art. 229.

The word " may " authorizes but does not provide that the Police Jury shall levy a tax. State ex rel vs. Police Jury, 40th Ann., 755.

ART. LV.---FINES AND BONDS FORFEITED TO BE COLLECTED FOR THE SUPPORT OF THE COMMON SCHOOLS.

SEC. 55. That all fines imposed by the several district courts for violation of law and the amount collected on all forfeited bonds in criminal cases, after deducting commissions, shall be paid over by the sheriff of the parish in which the same are imposed and collected, to the treasurers of the school boards in said parishes, and shall be applied to the support of the common schools, as are applied to other funds levied for the purpose (the parish of Orleans excepted).

ART. LVI.---SCHOOL TREASURER.

SEC. 56. That the parish treasurer in every parish (the parish of Orleans excepted) shall be and is constituted the treasurer of all school funds apportioned by the State to such parish, or raised, collected or donated therein for the support of the free public schools; he shall receive and receipt for all such funds to the Treasurer of the State, and to the collector of the parish taxes.

ART. LVII.--- BOND OF THE TREASURER.

SEC 57. That immediately upon the passage of this act, and thereafter before he enters upon the duties of his office, the parish treasurer of each parish who shall be elected after the passage of this act, shall, in addition to the bond required by existing law, execute a bond in favor of the Governor of the State, with good and solvent security, in a sum equal to the amount annually apportioned to the parish; the sureties on said bonds shall be residents of the parish, and shall own therein real estate worth over and above all incumbrance the amount of their obligations thereon; said bond must be accepted by the president of the Board of Directors, and the clerk of the district court, who shall record the same in the mortgage book of the parish, and shall forward to the State Superintendent of Education and to the State Treasurer a copy of said bond, with a certificate of its acceptance and registry endorsed thereon.

ART. LVIII.---TRANSFER OF SCHOOL FUNDS.

SEC. 58. That said treasurer, immediately upon the acceptance of his bond, shall demand of his predecessor in the office of the treasurer of the school funds, the custody of all books and papers and of all balances of school money in his hand as custodian of the school funds of the parish.

ART. LIX.---HOW THE SCHOOL FUNDS SHALL BE DISBURSED.

SEC. 59. That said treasurer shall pay out of the school funds intrusted in his charge only on warrants drawn by the president and countersigned by the secretary of the parish school board, and shall state against what school district fund it was drawn, which warrants shall be drawn by these officers only in virtue of appropriations regularly made by the parish board; the parish board shall make annually an estimate of the amount of revenue for the year, appropriating the same as above required, and no warrant beyond the amount estimated shall be drawn for any year. These warrants shall be numbered and shall specify on their face to whom and for what they are given, and the date of the appropriation made by the school board; the treasurer shall pay these warrants only to the extent of the amount to the credit on his books, and in the order in which they are presented, of school districts, in behalf of which the warrants shall have been drawn, and said warrant shall be filed in the office as vouchers, and with the account book kept by him as treasurer of the school fund shall always be subject to examination by any one who chooses to examine them.

ART. LX.—TREASURER'S COMPENSATION.

SEC. 60. That the compensation of the treasurer shall be a sum to be fixed by the State Board of Education, for each parish, according to its territorial area, and the amount of fund to be disbursed; but in no case shall it exceed two and a half per cent. on the amount disbursed by him as shown by his vouchers.

ART. LXI.—RECEIPTS AND DISBURSEMENTS. ACCOUNT OF WHEN REQUIRED AND HOW BE MADE.

SEC. 61. That it shall be the duty of the treasurer to furnish to the parish board accounts of his receipts and disbursements as often as required by them, and before the 10th day of January, annually he shall forward to the State Superintendent of Public Education, in such form as he shall prescribe, a full report of his receipts and disbursements for the year, and of the balance on hand to the credit of each ward or school district, and the indebtedness outstanding on the first day of January; provided, the foregoing sections do not apply to the treasurer of the board for the parish of Orleans.

ART. LXII.—CITY SCHOOLS.

SEC. 62. That all the public schools of the parish of Orleans, and the property and appurtenances thereof, shall be under the direction and control of a board of directors. Said board shall consist of twenty members, eight of whom shall be appointed by the Governor, by and with the consent and approval of the State board of education, and twelve members thereof shall be elected by the city council of New Orleans. The members of said board shall hold office during four years after their appointment and election, except as hereinafter provided, and until their successors are appointed or elected and qualified. On the first organization of said board by the members thereof, who shall be appointed and elected on the passage hereof, and in the manner aforesaid, the members shall be divided into four classes, by such method as they may choose, each class to consist of three members, elected by the city council and two members appointed by the Governor, by and with the consent and approval of the State board of education, whose terms shall expire respectively in one, two, three and four years, and whose successors shall be elected and appointed for four years, and in the manner set forth above; so that one-fourth of the membership of said board shall expire, and be elected and appointed annualy. Vacancies in membership shall be filled by the appointive or elective power, as herein provided.

ART. LXIII.—ORGANIZATION OF THE BOARD AND SALARY.

SEC. 63. That said board of directors of the public schools of the parish of Orleans shall be a body corporate in law, with power to sue and be sued. Eleven members shall constitute a quorum for the transaction of business. Legal process shall be served on the president; in his absence or inability to act, on the vice-president. The city attorney shall act as attorney for the board. The board shall be organized within ten days after its appointment, with a president and vice-president chosen from among its members, and a secretary, who shall not be a member of the board. The salary of the secretary shall not exceed the sum of eighteen hundred dollars ($1.800) per annum. In addition to the duties of his office, which may be fully prescribed by the board, he shall make a quarterly report to the State Superintendent of Education of the cost of maintaining the city schools, and shall keep the accounts of said board in such manner as to be in strict accordance with such budget as they may adopt, certifying to said board at each monthly meeting the expenses of said board for each current month. Said board shall have control of all buildings, records, papers, furniture and property of any kind pertaining to the administration of the schools, and shall have the management of all the public schools within the limits of the city of New Orleans. The expenses of said board for its stationery and other purposes shall not exceed twelve hundred dollars per annum, this limitation not to apply to the schools or teachers, but simply to the expenses of the board. The salary of the secretary shall be paid in the same manner as hereinafter provided for the payment of the salary of the superintendent.

ART. LXIV.–AUTHORITY OF THE DIRECTORS–PARISH OF ORLEANS.

Sec. 64. That in addition to the powers and duties hereinbefore granted to and imposed upon parish boards, the powers and duties of said board of directors of the parish of Orleans shall be as follows:

First. It shall adjust and fix equitably the salaries of teachers and porters or portresses employed in the schools, and of the secretary and employees and of such assistant superintendents as it may deem necessary for an efficient supervision of the schools.

Second. It shall limit the annual expenses of maintaining the schools to the annual revenue, and the expense for any one month shall not exceed the one-ninth part of the whole amount provided for the schools.

Third. It shall prescribe rules for subjecting teachers, or candidates for teacherships, to a careful competitive examination on all such branches as they are expected to teach, and no person shall be elected to a position as teacher without a favorable report on his or her moral and mental qualifications by an organized committee of examiners appointed by the board. Teachers regularly examined and elected shall not be removed from the schools during the time for which employed, except on, written charges of immorality, neglect of duty, incompetency or malfeasance, of which he or she shall have been found guilty by a majority of the members of the board at a regular monthly meeting. The said board may except from such examination any person

who has passed a satisfactory examination, as required by Act
No. 23 of eighteen hundred and seventy seven, approved March
twenty-sixth (26th), eighteen hundred and seventy seven (18.7),
and who holds a certificate of qualification, and who h is had two
years or more experience as a teacher, so that the calling of a
teacher shall be elevated to a profession. and that a system of
life certificates shall be issued to all such teachers in the city of
New Orleans by the board of directors of city schools; any person who is a graduate of a State normal school, or of any college
or university duly authorized to confer degrees, certificates of
qualifications shall be given to all persons who successfully pass
such examination.

Fourth. It shall elect all teachers from among the candidates
holding certificates in the order of their merit, as shown by such
examination, including graduates of normal schools, as shown by
the averages attained at their final examinations, or from among
persons excepted from examination as hereinbefore provided.

Fifth. All certificates to teachers granted hereafter shall
stand good for three years; upon a second examination at the
end of three years, certificates of a higher grade shall be given, to
be good for five years, if the applicant is found competent to
teach a higher grade school than the one for which the first certificate issued.

Sixth. It shall hold regular monthly meetings on a day fixed
by it.

Seventh. It shall declare vacant the position of any of its
members who shall have failed to perform the duties assigned to
him, or have absented himself from two successive monthly meetings of the board without leave, or have been guilty of any breach
of decorum, or of any other act inconsistent with the dignity of a
school director; and it shall report each vacancy to the body by
which the delinquent member shall have been previously elected
or appointed; it shall be the duty of the board of directors of
city schools elected and appointed under the provisions of this
act to examine and scrutinize personally the accounts of their
predecessors, in order to find out if their administration of the
school funds, committed to their charge for disbursement, has
been in accordance with law, so that in the future a proper administration of the city school fund may be had.

Eighth. It may establish, when practicable, evening or night
schools for the instruction of such youths as are prevented by
their daily vocations from receiving instruction during the day.

Ninth It may establish, when deemed advisable, one or more
normal schools or departments for the professional training and
improvement of candidates for teacherships, including, in the
course of instruction and training, lectures in the natural sciences,
and on the method of teaching and disciplining children, and the
practical exercise of non-teaching students in model classes
organized for that purpose by the faculty of the institution. To
graduates of these normal schools or departments, and also to
proficient students in other city schools of an academic grade,

the board may, in its discretion, award diplomas; and the graduates of the normal schools or departments who shall have been examined and found proficient in all the branches required to be taught in the public grammar schools, may be deemed preferred candidates for vacant positions in the city public schools, and the diplomas awarded to such graduates shall be deemed equivalent to teaching certificates of the highest grade for common schools; provided, that the final examinations for graduation from said normal schools, and upon which diplomas may be awarded, shall be conducted in the same manner and include the same subjects as the public competitive examinations required by paragraph three (3) of this section.

ART. LXV.   SERVICES OF CITY BOARD SHALL BE RENDERED
WITHOUT COMPENSATION.

SEC. 65.   That no school director of the city of New Orleans shall receive compensation for his services as a school director.

ART. LXVI —SUPERINTENDENT OF NEW ORLEANS CITY SCHOOLS,
HIS DUTIES, AUTHORITY, SALARY.

SEC. 66.   That the said board is authorized to appoint for the constant supervision and periodical examination of the public schools of the parish of Orleans, a competent and experienced educator to be designated as superintedent.   He shall aid the directors in organizing the schools and in improving the methods of instruction therein. in examining candidates for teacherships, and in conducting periodical examinations of pupils for promotion through the respective grades of the schools, and in maintaining general uniformity and discipline in the management of all the schools.   He shall make semi annual reports on the condition and needs of the schools to the said board, and an annual report on or before the first of January to the State Board of Education, as hereinbefore required ; and, whenever notified to be present, he shall attend meetings of the State Board of Education.   The superintendent shall receive an annual salary of two thousand dollars, payable in equal monthly installments, payable on the roll of the board of directors of city schools in the same manner and at the same time that the employées and expenses of said board of directors are paid.   He shall hold his office for the term of four years, subject to removal by the board for neglect of duty or malfeasance, of which, after an impartial hearing by the board, he shall have been adjudged guilty.   He shall be ex-officio a member of said board, and entitled to participate in its deliberations and debates, and in the examinations of candidates for teacherships, but he shall not cast a vote in the board.

ART. LXVII.—TREASURER OF NEW ORLEANS—EX-OFFICIO TREASURER
OF THE BOARD.—HIS BOND.

SEC. 67.   That the Treasurer of New Orleans shall ex-officio be the treasurer of said board and shall receive all funds apportioned by the State to such city, or received or collected for the support of the free public schools from any and all sources. He shall give bond, with good and solvent security, in the sum of ten thousand dollars ($10,000) in favor of the president of said board and his successors in office, to be accepted and approved by said board and recorded in the mortgage office of the parish, and which bond shall then be filed and kept on record in the office of the said board. The filing of said bond, and taking and filing the usual oath of office before any officer authorized to administer the same, shall qualify the treasurer to act.

ART. LXVIII.—TREASURER'S OFFICE, REMOVAL, SUCCESSOR, SALARY.

SEC. 68. That said treasurer shall hold his office for four years, or during his term of office as City Treasurer, unless sooner removed after due trial and hearing by the said board, for neglect of duty or malfeasance in office; and in case of removal by the board, it shall elect a treasurer who shall not be a member. He shall receive the sum of six hundred dollars per annum for the trouble and expenses which may be incurred by him in the discharge of the duties imposed under this act, payable monthly on his own warrant, as hereinbefore provided for the payment of the superintendent's salary. He shall keep his office open at all such times as may be prescribed by said board, for the payment of pay-rolls or checks in favor of teachers and other employees of the board.

ART. LXIX.—EX-OFFICIO MEMBERS.

SEC. 69. That the Mayor, Treasurer and Comptroller of the city of New Orleans shall be ex-officio members of the said board and be entitled to take part in all the debates and deliberations in said board on the ways and means for maintaining the public schools of said parish, but they shall not have the right to vote.

ART. LXX.—REPORT OF THE BOARD, WHEN AND TO WHOM MADE, ITS CONTENTS.

SEC. 70. That in addition to the duties imposed upon boards of school directors, it shall be the duty of said board for the parish of Orleans to present to the Common Council of the city of New Orleans, on the first day of December of each year, a full report of the condition of the city schools, showing the number of teachers and other employees and their salaries; the number and location of school houses, with the condition thereof, and the estimated cost of keeping all appurtenant grounds in good repair during the ensuing year; also a detailed exhibit of all receipts and expenditures of the board for the schools during the previous twelve months; said report shall be accompanied with a statement certified by the officers of the board of the average daily tendance of pupils during the annual session, and the average expense per capita of their instruction.

ART. LXXI.—BUDGET OF ANNUAL EXPENSES.—WHAT IT
SHALL INCLUDE.

SEC. 71. That it shall be the duty of the Common Council of the city of New Orleans, in making up their budget of annual expenses, to include therein the amount necessary to meet the expenses of the schools, as shown by the statement of the actual attendance, and cost of instruction required by the preceeding section, with such additional allowance for probable increased attendance and contingent expenses as may seem just and reasonable to the City Council, and to keep in good repair all school houses and school grounds belonging to the city; provided, that the sum appropriated with the probable receipts from the State school fund and poll tax shall not exceed the aggregate amount required for the maintenance of the schools during the year, and for the keeping in good repair all school houses and school grounds belonging to the city, as shown by the statement of the school board; and, provided further, that the amount to be appropriated by said city shall not be less than the sum of two hundred and fifty thousand dollars; of said amount so to be appropriated by said City Council, not less than the sum of one hundred and seventy-five thousand dollars shall be provided for in the annual city budget of expenditures, and the balance out of the reserve fund of twenty per cent., constituted by Section 66 of Act No. 20, approved June twenty-third, eighteen hundred and eighty-two, and by Act No. one hundred and nine, of eighteen hundred and eighty-six, and said balance is hereby constituted a first lien and claim against said reserve fund, and shall be paid out of the first collection made on account of the same and by preference over all claims whatsoever; provided further, that out of the amount so appropriated by said city, said board of directors shall, in the year eighteen hundred and eighty-nine (1889), and annually for five years thereafter, appropriate a sum sufficient to extinguish at least one-sixth of the unpaid claims against said board for the years eighteen hundred and eighty, eighteen hundred and eighty-one, eighteen hundred and eighty-two and eighteen hundred and eighty-four, so that said claims shall be entirely paid by the beginning of the year eighteen hundred and ninety-five. The board of directors for the parish of Orleans are hereby authorized to enforce the provisions of this section by the application to a court of competent jurisdiction, by a writ of mandamus or other effective remedy.

" The City of New Orleans is, in the absence of Constitutional provision with reference to the public schools, in so far as relates to its budget, not subject to interference on the part of the General Assembly, and cannot be made to set aside the amount mentioned in this section." See case of the School Board of Directors vs. the City of New Orleans, 42nd Ann.—

ART. LXXII.-PROVISIONS FOR AFFORDING PROPER EVIDENCE OF CLAIM.

SEC. 72. That for the purpose of affording proper evidence of said claims aforesaid (and for no other purpose whatsoever), said board shall issue certificates of indebtedness to an amount equal to the total amount of said claims and maturing in six equal instalments on the first day of January, eighteen hundred and ninety, eighteen hundred and ninety-one, eighteen hundred and ninety-two, eighteen hundred and ninety-three, eighteen hundred and ninety four and eighteen hundred and ninety-five.

ART. LXXIII.-RESTRICTIONS ON CONTRACTS AND DEBTS.

SEC. 73. That the different boards of directors shall not be empowered to make contracts or debts for any one year greater the amount of revenue provided for according to this act, it being the intent hereof that parties contracting with said board shall take heed that due revenue shall have been provided to satisfy the claim, otherwise they may lose and forfeit the same, and no action or execution shall be allowed in aid thereof, and that the board shall not exceed their powers in incurring the debt.

ART. LXXIV.—APPEAL OF ALL CONFLICTING CLAUSES.

SEC. 74. That this act shall go into effect from and after its passage; and nothing in this act shall be so construed as to vacate the office of any teacher until the expiration of the term for which he or she shall have been appointed under existing laws, nor as requiring such persons now teaching in the public schools of the city of New Orleans to qualify in accordance with this act, or to pass such examinations as are otherwise demanded by paragraph five of section sixty-four, and that all laws in conflict with the provisions of this act be, and the same are hereby repealed, except acts passed at the present session of the General Assembly.

LAWS DATED PREVIOUS TO GENERAL ACT No. 81, OF THE YEAR 1888, STILL IN FORCE AND AUXILIARY TO THAT ACT.

ACT NO. 82, APPROVED APRIL 9, 1873.

ART. LXXV. — STATE AND PARISH BOARDS CANNOT BE COMPELLED TO GIVE BOND AND SECURITY IN SUITS.

SEC 4. In all judicial proceedings where, by law, bond and security are required from litigants, the State Board of Education shall be dispensed from furnishing bond or security; and in all suits in which the State or parish board of education may be plaintiffs, defendants, intervenors, garnishees, or interested in any manner whatsoever, it shall be the duty of the court before whom such suits are pending, on the affidavit of the attorney representing the State or parish board of education, if the case is one of serious public interest and in which a speedy decision is desirable, to set the cause for trial by preference, and all such cases may also be fixed for trial as early as possible on motion or petition of the attorney of the State or parish board of education.

ACT NO. 122, OF APRIL 7, 1874.

ART. LXXVI. — ATTORNEYS MAY BE APPOINTED TO PROTECT SCHOOL INTERESTS.

SEC. 7. The Superintendent of Public Education may appoint a person of legal attainments in each school division (parish) of the State, to examine notes due and other assets arising out of purchase of lands granted to educational purposes; to recover lands improperly held and revenues diverted, and generally protect the school interests in matters appertaining thereto. He (the attorney) shall be paid a commission on moneys recovered, not exceeding ten per cent, and on the value of lands and other property recovered, not exceeding five per cent.

ACT 1868; SEC. 1304, OF REVISED STATUTES.

ART. LXXVII.— RIGHTS OF FREE PASSAGE OVER STREAMS, ETC.

The free right of passage or conveyance, over all public ferries, bridges and roads (except the ferries of the Mississippi River) which are rented out by the State or parish, or over which the State or parish exercises any control, or for which license is paid or toll exacted, be and is hereby granted to all children on foot attending free public schools, and no tolls or fees shall be demanded or exacted from said children by the keepers or attendants of said ferries, bridges or roads in their passage to and from schools between the hours of 7 o'clock A. M. and 9 o'clock A. M., and *four* o'clock P. M. and *six* o'clock P. M.; *provided*, that on Sundays and holidays no scholar shall have the right to cross such ferries, bridges or roads on terms different from those of any ordinary passenger.

ACT 23, APPROVED MARCH 26, 1877.

SEC. 2 OF ACT 70, APPROVED JULY 1, 1882.

ART. LXXVIII.—NEGOTIABLE EVIDENCE OF DEBTS CANNOT BE ISSUED.

SEC. 2. (Extract). "Said board shall have no power to issue negotiable evidences of debt."

ART. LXXIX.—INDEBTEDNESS OF PARISH SCHOOL BOARDS, LIMITED.

SEC. 5 of Act 23 of 1877. The parish school board shall limit the aggregate annual expense of accommodating and maintaining the free public schools of the parish to the amount of the revenue derived from the State, parish and such donations as shall be made by public-spirited citizens for or toward the support thereof.

(Extract). Section 6 of Act 70, of the year 1882.—No school of less than ten pupils shall be opened or maintained in any locality; nor shall more than forty pupils be placed in charge of any one teacher.

ACT 96, OF THE YEAR 1877.

RELATIVE TO THE POLL TAX AND OTHER LAWS RESPECTING THE REVENUES FOR SCHOOLS.

ACT 96, APPROVED APRIL 20, 1877.

ART. LXXX.—ASSESSOR.—ANNUAL ENUMERATION OF YOUTHS.

SEC. 40. It is the duty of the assessors (Orleans excepted), on or before the 10th day of November, 1877, and every two years thereafter, to make an accurate enumeration of all the youths of their respective parishes between the ages of six and twenty-one years, designating distinctly the number of each sex between those ages in each of the school districts or wards into which the parish may be divided; the assessor shall make out duplicate lists of the enumeration so made, and deliver one to the president of the board of school directors and the other he shall immediately transmit to the State Superintendent of Public Education.

The assessor shall make an accurate enumeration of the white children between six and eighteen years and of the colored children between six and eighteen years. Act 85 of the year 1888, Sec. 16.

ACT 81, APPROVED JULY 12, 1888.

ART. LXXXI.—PARISH SUPERINTENDENT'S DUTY RESPECTING ENUMERATION OF YOUTHS.

SEC. 29. Makes it the duty of each parish superintendent, on or before the 10th day of January of each year, to furnish the State Superintendent a report showing the number of children between six and eighteen years residing in the parish, and the whole number residing in each district designated by its number.

LAWS RELATIVE TO RAISING REVENUE FOR THE MAINTENANCE OF THE FREE PUBLIC SCHOOLS.

ART. LXXXII.—POLL TAX.

The General Assembly shall levy an annual poll tax for the maintenance of public schools upon every male inhabitant in the State over the age of twenty one years, which shall never be less than one dollar nor exceed one dollar and a half *per capita*—and the General Assembly shall pass laws to enforce payment of the said tax. Constitution 208.

The poll tax list rendered by the Assessor to the Parish School Board, should constitute the basis for settlement between the Sheriff and the School Board. [Act No. 89, of 1888.]

The Sheriff should account for full amount of Poll Tax roll; and has the right to credits as follows, and no other, to-wit:

Poll taxes collected and paid to proper officer, poll taxes collected by clerk of court, poll taxes of non-residents and those from whom it is not possible to collect, with due diligence.

Quarterly settlements are due by the Tax Collector, also an annual statement. [Sections 5 and 6 of Act No. 120, of 1880.]

DELAYS SHOULD NOT BE GRANTED

The school authorities in the parishes are without authority to grant delays to the Tax Collectors. [31 Ann., 423.]

The powers granted to collect poll taxes are exceptional.

"That the said poll tax shall operate as a first privilege and "lien on all the real and personal property, of whatever kind, "which may be owned by and to which the said tax-payer may "have any right for the year he may owe the tax. [Section No. 2, Act No. 120, 1880.]

The third Section was repealed *Vide* Act 61, of 1882.

COLLECTOR'S BOOK—RESPECTING THE POLL TAX.

"That the collector of the poll tax shall keep a book in which "he shall enter the tax as paid. He shall, in said book, give the "name of the party paying or for whom the tax is paid, the date "of the payment and by whom paid, and the amount paid,which "entry shall be made when the payment is made, or within three "days, and all payments shall be entered in the books prior to "settlement—on making settlements the collector shall by his "affidavit establish compliance." [Section 4, Act 120, of 1880.]

Quietus can be given only by the School Boards, in so far as relates to the poll tax.

RULE TO SHOW CAUSE.

The sheriff can be made to show cause why the poll tax has not been collected. The rule can be heard at chambers after three days' service. [Act 89, of 1888.]

ACT 120, APPROVED APRIL 10, 1880.

ART. LXXXIII.—LIMIT OF POLL TAX.

From each inhabitant over the age of twenty-one years, not attached to the army or navy of the United States, there shall be collected annually the sum of one dollar as poll tax. R. S. 1325.

ACT 89, APPROVED JULY 12, 1888.

REQUIRING THE ASSESSORS TO RENDER A SCHE-
DULE LIST BY WARDS AND REQUIRING
THE SHERIFF TO COLLECT SAID LIST
OR TO SHOW CAUSE WHY
NOT COLLECTED.

ART. LXXXIV.—COLLECTION OF THE POLL TAX.

SEC. 1. The assessors are required to render to the school boards of their respective parishes, annually, by the first Satur-day of October, a complete schedule list, by wards, of all persons liable to pay a poll tax in their respective parishes. If any as-sessor fails to comply with the requirement of this act, the fail-ure shall be cause for removal; besides, he shall be subject to a fine of $250, for the benefit of the public schools in the parish in which the delinquent officer resides, and in which he is the as-sessor. In the city of New Orleans the board of assessors shall comply with the requirement of this act, and in the event of failure, shall be subject to dismissal and penalty as before pro-vided.

ART. LXXXV.—RETURN OF COLLECTIONS TO BE MADE BY THE SHERIFFS AND TAX COLLECTORS.

SEC. 2. That the sheriffs and tax collectors in their respective parishes shall return, by the first Saturday of February, of each and every year, to the school boards of their respective parishes, a list predicated upon the list before mentioned by wards, show-ing all persons in the parishes respectively, who have paid their poll tax, as well as persons who have not paid the same, and shall return their reasons in writing and under oath, the cause in each instance of the non-payment of a poll tax, and why they have not collected the tax not collected.

ART. LXXXVI.—PENALTIES.

SEC. 3. If the said sheriff or tax collector fails to show cause why the said poll tax has not been collected, he shall be respon-sible for and shall pay the poll taxes he has failed to collect, and shall be held liable with his securities on his official bond for the payment of said tax.

ART. LXXXVII.--RULE TO SHOW CAUSE OF NON-COMPLIANCE.

SEC. 4. That the sheriff can be made to show cause why the said poll tax has not been collected, at chambers, before the district judge, after service of rule and three days have elapsed after service.

ACT 87, APPROVED JULY 8, 1886.

RECEIPT FOR POLL TAX REQUIRED.

AN ACT TO PROVIDE FOR THE BETTER AND MORE SPEEDY COLLECTION OF THE POLL TAX.

ART. LXXXVIII.---RECEIPT REQUIRED.

SEC. 1. Before persons serving as jurors or as witnesses in criminal cases shall receive the compensation to which they are entitled for their mileage and per diem, they shall exhibit to the clerk of the court a receipt for the poll tax or taxes due by them.

ART. LXXXIX.--TAX (POLL) TO BE DEDUCTED IF RECEIPT BE NOT PRODUCED.

SEC. 2. On their failure to produce such receipt the clerk of the court, or other officer, issuing certificates or warrants for their *mileage* and *per diem*, shall issue certificates or warrants for amount less the poll tax due, and shall issue the certificate or warrants for amount so reserved for poll tax, to the treasurer of the school board of the parish, who shall collect same.

ART. XC.---REPORT TO BE MADE BY THE CLERK OF COURT OR OTHER OFFICER.

SEC. 3. The clerk of court or other officer, issuing such certificates or warrants, shall report to the tax collector of the parish the names of all persons from whom he has reserved amounts for poll tax, and the tax collector shall give such person credit for such poll tax.

ART. XCI.—REVENUES FROM LOCAL TAXATION.

In addition, the revenue system adopted, provides for local taxation. Vide Sec. 54, of Act 81, of 1888.

ART. XCII.—GENERAL REVENUE ACT.

THE GENERAL REVENUE ACT No. 85 APPROVED JULY 12, 1888, PROVIDES.

SEC. 89. (Third paragraph.) One and one-eighth mills public education tax for the purpose :

1st. To pay the interest on the free school fund, under Article 233 of the Constitution.

2nd. To pay the interest on the seminary fund under the second clause of said article

3rd. To pay the interest on the Mechanical and Agricultural College fund, under the 3rd clause of said article of the Constitution.

The remainder of said public education tax shall be applied to the establishment, maintenance and support of the free public schools throughout the State. Articles 224, to 233 inclusive of the State Constitution.

Total valuation of property in the State subject to valuation is $226,392 17 for 1889, Auditor's report for 1889. The $1\frac{1}{4}$ mills calculated on this amount will amount to considerably less than the three hundred thousand dollars appropriated.

ACT 124, APPROVED JULY 6, 1882.

TO PERMIT DONATIONS *MORTIS CAUSA* AND *INTER VIVOS* TO BE MADE.

ART. XCIII.—DONATIONS FOR EDUCATIONAL, CHARITABLE OR LITERARY PURPOSES.

An act to permit donations *mortis causa* or *inter vivos* to be made to trustees for educational, charitable or literary purposes, or for the benefit of educational, literary or charitable institutions, already existing or to be founded; providing that such trustees shall constitute a body corporate, and the manner of their incorporation; regulating the powers, duties and action of such trustees and exempting all donations made for the purposes and in the manner provided in this act, from the provisions of the laws of the State relative to substitution, trusts and *fidei commissæ;* provided, that nothing shall be considered as affecting the law relative to the disposable portion.

ART. XCIV. DONORS.

SEC. 1. Any one can make a donation of any description of property and to any amount to trustees for educational, charitable or literary purposes, or for the benefit of educational, charitable or literary institutions whether already existing, or thereafter to be founded.

ART. XCV.—CONDITIONS THE DONOR CAN IMPOSE.

SEC. 2. The donor shall have the right to prescribe the number of trustees; the causes for which the trustees shall cease to be such; the manner in which vacancies shall be filled and the manner and formalities the trustees shall follow in transacting business.

ART. XCVI.—PROPERTY CANNOT BE MADE INALIENABLE.

SEC. 3. The donor shall have the right to prescribe the manner in which the property donated shall be administered, and the objects to which it or any part thereof, or the revenues thereof, shall be applied; provided, however, that property donated cannot be made inalienable; but the donor thereof shall have the right to prescribe in what manner and under what circumstances the trustees shall be empowered to sell the same, or any portion thereof, or to change any investment once made.

ART. XCVII.—TRUSTEES TO ORGANIZE IN A BODY CORPORATE.

SEC. 4. That the trustees named in the act of donation and their successors or substitutes, or such of them as are willing and may accept the trust, shall, upon complying with the laws of this State, relative to the organization of corporations for literary, scientific, religious and charitable purposes, constitute a body corporate with the power of continuous succession and unlimited duration, and with all the powers conferred upon corporations by said law or by custom, provided, however, that the requirement of said law, as to the number of persons necessary for the formation of a corporation, shall not apply to such trustees; and provided further, that if any of the trustees will not or can not accept the trust, then such of those named as are willing, may accept, and, in the manner prescribed in the act of donation, proceed to fill the vacancies up to the required number.

ART. XCVIII.—GOVERNOR MAY, WHENEVER THERE IS A FAILURE ON THE PART OF TRUSTEES TO ACCEPT, APPOINT OTHERS.

SEC. 5. That whenever there is an entire failure of the trustees to accept, the Governor of the State may name a number of persons equal to the number named by the donor, and who shall fill the places of, and be vested with all the powers conferred upon the trustees by said donor.

ART. XCIX.—DUTY OF THE TRUSTEES.

SEC. 6. The board of trustees shall administer the property entrusted to them in conformity with the directions contained in the act of donation, and shall have all the powers needed in such administration; but cannot mortgage nor encumber the donated property, except as may be prescribed in the act of donation. And said trustees shall not be entitled to any remuneration for their services, unless expressly granted in the act of donation.

ART. C.—DUTY OF THE TRUSTEES RESPECTING OTHER DONATIONS.

SEC. 7. Said board of trustees shall have the power to accept and administer other donations *mortis causa* or *inter vivos* from the same or other, and to apply the same as may be prescribed in the subsequent act of donation The administration of such subsequent act of donations, to be governed by the directions contained in the subsequent act of donation.

ART. CI —FIDEI COMMISSÆ.

SEC. 8. The provisions contained in the Revised Civil Code, or other laws of the State relative to substitutions *fidei commissæ* or trust dispositions, shall not be deemed to apply to, or in any manner affect donations made for the purposes and in the manner provided by this act, and all laws or parts of laws conflicting with the provisions of this act, are repealed in so far as regards the purposes of this act, but not otherwise.

LAWS OF THE UNITED STATES RELATIVE TO DONATIONS MADE BY THE U. S. GOVERNMENT.

UNITED STATES STATUTES AT LARGE, VOL. 4, CHAPTER LXXXIII, PAGE 179.

ART CII.—FREE SCHOOLS.—DONATION.

SEC. 1. There was allowed to Louisiana and other States, over what each State was entitled to by the terms of the compact entered into, between them and the United States, upon their admission into the Union ; ten per cent of the net proceeds of the sales of the public lands thereafter to be made within the limits of each State respectively.

ART. CIII.—DONATION ACCORDING TO FEDERAL REPRESENTATION.

SEC. 2. After the deduction of the ten per cent., and the salaries and expenses of the general land office, expenses for surveying public lands, salaries of the registers and receivers and expenses of their offices: the 5% to new States of all the public lands of the United States, wherever situated which were sold subsequent to the 31st of December, 1841; the remainder shall be divided among the twenty six States of the Union according to their respective federal representative population as ascertained by the last census, to be applied by the legislature of the said States to such purposes as the legislature may direct.

ART. CIV. — ACT OF THE CONGRESS OF THE UNITED STATES, APPROVED FEBRUARY 15, 1843. — STATUTES AT LARGE, VOL. 5, PAGE 600.

SEC. 1. Authorized the sale of lands previously reserved and appropriated by Congress for the use of schools, within the State of Louisiana, also to invest the money arising from the sales thereof in some productive fund, that the proceeds are to be applied under the direction of the legislature to the support of schools within the several townships and district of country for which they were originally reserved, and for no other purpose. They are to be sold with the consent of the inhabitants of the township or district in the manner directed by the legislature, and in the apportionment of the proceeds each township and district is entitled to the sum or sums and no more, arising from the sale of the school lands of such township or district.

ART. CV. — LEASE OF LAND.

SEC. 2. The legislature is authorized to protect these lands from injury and waste and to lease same, (if not deemed expedient to sell them) for any term not exceeding four years.

ART. CVI. — FUNDS CAN BE INVESTED BY LEGISLATIVE AUTHORITY.

SEC. 3. Investment of the funds accruing to any township or district authorized in certain contingency.

ART. CVII.—STATE, A TRUSTEE.

NOTE. The State is a trustee of these lands or of the proceeds of their sale for the use of the inhabitants of the township in which they are located—*vide*, Board of School Directors vs. Ober. 32 A. 419.

EDUCATIONAL LAND GRANTS BY THE UNITED STATES TO LOUISIANA AND OTHER STATES TO JUNE 30, 1880.

GRANTS AND RESERVATIONS.

The lands granted in the States and reserved in the Territories for educational purposes by acts of Congress from 1785 to June 30, 1880, were—

FOR PUBLIC OR COMMON SCHOOLS.

Every sixteenth section of public land in the States admitted prior to 1848, and every sixteenth and thirty-sixth section of such land in States and Territories since organized—estimated at 67,893,919 acres.

FOR SEMINARIES OR UNIVERSITIES.

The quantity of two townships, or 46,080 acres, in each State or Territory containing public land, and, in some instances, a greater quantity, for the support of seminaries or schools of a higher grade—estimated at 1,165,520 acres.

FOR AGRICULTURAL AND MECHANICAL COLLEGES.

The grant to all the States for agricultural and mechanical colleges, by act of July 2, 1862, and its supplements, of 30,000 acres, for each Representative and Senator in Congress to which the State was entitled, of land "in place" where the State contained a sufficient quantity of public land subject to sale at ordinary private entry at the rate of $1.25 per acre, and of scrip representing an equal number of acres where the State did not contain such description of land, the scrip to be sold by the State and located by its assignees on any such land in other States and Territories, subject to certain restrictions. Land in place, 1,770,000 acres; land scrip, 7.830,000; total, 9,600,000 acres.

In all, 78,659,439 acres for educational purposes under the heads above set out to June 30, 1880.

The lands thus ceded to the several States were disposed of or are held for disposition, and the proceeds used as permanent endowments for common school funds. [See Reports of the Commissioner of Education, Hon. John Eaton, to June 30, 1880; land and auditor's reports of the several land States; Kiddle & Schem's Dictionary of Education; and also ninth census, E. A. Walker, Superintendent, for details of endowments of the several States for common schools resulting from the sales of United States land grants for education]. As an illustration, the State of Ohio has a permanent endowment for education, called the "Irreducible State Debt," the result of sale of all granted lands for education, of $4,289,718 52.

EARLY EDUCATIONAL INTEREST.

The importance attached to education by the founders of the Republic is shown by the provisions they made for its permanent endowment. Indeed, in the earliest settlements on this continent of the Anglo-Americans, measures were adopted in the cause of education, not only as essential to morals, social order, and individual happiness, but as necessary to new and liberal institutions. Every emigrant ship had its school-master on board, each settlement erected its school-house, and the cultivation of the mind advanced with the culture of the soil from the landing of the Mayflower through our colonial history.

Prior to the revolution, in the different colonies the subject of popular education had attracted attention, and provision had been made for its practical realization. The theory of general education found no basis in the aristocratic constitution of the mother country, while in the colonies themselves were to be found influences decidedly hostile to it. The injustice and persecution, however, which had caused the immigration to this country, especially to the northern colonies, wonderfully neutralized the religious and political prejudices of the pilgrims, and prepared them to accept doctrines of very opposite tendency. The comparative feebleness of aristocratic prestige in the forests of the New World permitted the development of independent

manhood.   The establishment of democracy was followed by the
natural development of its principles, especially in the direction
of popular education.

After the erection of the States into an independent republic,
and before the adoption of the constitution, the Continental Congress, by the ordinance of the 20th of May, 1785, respecting the
disposition of lands in the Western Territory, prepared the way
for the advance of settlements and education as contempo-
raneous interests.

THE FIRST RESERVATION FOR SCHOOL PURPOSES — THE SIX-
TEENTH SECTION.

Mr. Jefferson, Mr. Dane, Mr. Madison, and other statesmen of
that day assumed, without question, that a government, as the
organ of society, enjoys the right, and is vested with the power,
to meet the necessity of public education.   So the question of endowment of educational institutions by the Government in aid of
the cause of education seems to have met no serious opposition
in the Congress of the Confederation, and no member raised his
voice against this vital and essential provision relating to it in
the ordinance of May 20th, 1785, " for ascertaining the mode of
disposing of lands in the Western Territory."   This provided :
" There shall be reserved the lot No. 16 of every township for the
maintenance of public schools within said township."

This was an endowment of 640 acres of land [one section of
land one mile square] in a township 6 miles square, for the support and maintenance of public schools " within said township."
The manner of establishment of public schools thereunder, and by
whom, was not mentioned.   It was a reservation by the United
States, and advanced and established a principle which finally
dedicated one thirty-sixth part of all public lands of the United
States, with certain exception as to mineral, etc., to the cause of
education by public schools.

July 23, 1787, in the report from a committee consisting of
Messrs. Carrington, Kinm, Dane, Madison and Benson, reporting
an ordinance of " Powers to the Board of Treasury " to contract
for the sale of western territory in the Continental Congress, it
was ordered " That the lot No. 16 in each township, or fractional
part of a township, to be given perpetually for the purpose contained in said ordinance " [the ordinance of May 20, 1785, above
referred to].   This additional legislation made the reservation of
the sixteenth section perpetual.

In the Continental Congress, July 13, 1787, according to order,
the ordinance for the government of the " Territory of the United
States northwest of the river Ohio " came on, was read a third
time, and passed.   It contained the following :

ART. 3.   Religion, morality, and knowledge being necessary to
good government, and the happiness of mankind, schools and the
means of education shall forever be encouraged.

The provision of the ordinance of May 20, 1785, relating to the reservation of the sixteenth section in every township of public land, was the inception of the present rule of reservation of certain sections of land for school purposes.

The endowment was the subject of much legislation in the years following. The question was raised that there was no reason why the United States should not organize, control and manage these public schools so endowed. The reservation of lands was made by surveyors and duly returned.

This policy at once met with enthusiastic approval from the public, and was tacitly incorporated into the American system as one of its fundamental organic ideas. Whether the public schools thus endowed by the United States were to be National or State control remained a question, and the lands were held in reservation merely, until after the admission of the State of Ohio, in 1802.

The movement in the cause of education was not confined to the legislative department, for at any early period the public mind was aroused to an importance of the subject by elaborate papers emanating from eminent men, among whom stands conspicuous Dr Benjamin Rush, one of the signers of the Declaration of Independence, who in 1786 memorialized the legislature of Pennsylvania in favor of a thorough system of popular instruction, maintaining that it was favorable to liberty, as freedom could only exist in the society of knowledge; that it favors just ideas of law and government; that it fosters agriculture, the basis of national wealth; that manufactures of all kinds owe their perfection chiefly to learning; that its beneficial influence is thus made co-extensive with the entire scope of man's being, mortal and immortal, individual and social. At a later period, 1790, the same great man addressed a Congressional representative from Pennsylvania, declaring that "the attempts to perpetuate our existence as a free people by establishing the means of national credit and defense" are "feeble bulwarks against slavery compared with the habits of labor and virtue disseminated among our people;" adding, "Let us establish schools for that purpose in every township in the United States, and conform them to reason, humanity, and the state of society in America," and then will "the generations which are to follow us realize the precious ideas of the dignity and excellence of republican forms of government."

RESERVATION OF THE THIRTY SIXTH SECTION IN ADDITION TO THE SIXTEENTH.

The reservation of a section, or one mile square, of 640 acres, in each township, for the support of public schools, was specially provided for in the organization of each new State and Territory up to the time of the organization of Oregon Territory.

April 30, 1802, Congress, in the act authorizing the formation of a State government in the eastern portion of the Northwestern Territory (Ohio), enacted the following three propositions, which were offered for the acceptance or rejection of the convention to

form the constitution of Ohio. (Up to this time no transfer by
the United States or title or control of the sixteenth section of
reserved school lands had taken place).

By Section 7.

First. That the section number sixteen in every township,
and where such section has been sold, granted or disposed, or
other lands equivalent thereto and most contiguous to the same,
shall be granted to the inhabitants of such townships for the use
of schools.

The second was a saline reservation; and the third related to a
moiety of the net proceeds of the sale of public lands, for the
laying out of roads, etc.

The three conditions above set out were in consideration of the
non-taxation of the public domain, for a period after sale about
which there was serious discussion as to who should tax, or
whether it should be taxed at all. prior to or after purchase. The
non-taxation compensation was that no tax on the land sold by
the United States, should be laid by the authority of the States,
county or townships therein for the term of five years after the
date of sale. The object of this stipulation was to prevent any
person from obtaining a tax title under the authority of the State
before the United States had received the full amount of the purchase money. Lands were then sold on credit by the United
States of one, two, three, four and five years, at two dollars per
acre. The people of Ohio complied with the above stipulations,
November 29, 1802, and were admitted into the Union.

The act of Congress of March 3, 1803, in addition to the above
act of April 30, 1802, provided—

That the following several tracts of land in the State of Ohio
be, and the same are hereby, appropriated for the use of schools
in that State, and shall together with all the tracts of land heretofore appropriated for that purpose, be vested in the legislature
of that State, in trust for the use aforesaid, and for no other use,
intent, or purpose whatever.

Thus Congress transferred the reserved school lands, section
16 in each township, and provided an indemnity for such sections as had already been sold or taken prior to survey of the
State of Ohio, in trust for the United States, and the people of
the Sate for schools. Prior to this, laws were silent as to how
the proceeds of these reserved lands were to be applied, or by
whom.

Congress thus made the State its trustee. Compacts between
the United States on the admission of the States of Indiana. Illi-
nois and Louisiana, and all the States admitted into the Union
prior to 1820, also contained the provisions above set out.

THE SIXTEENTH SECTION.

To each organized Territory, after 1803, was and now is reserved the sixteenth section (until after the Oregon Territory act
reserved the thirty sixth as well) for school purposes, which reservation is carried into grant and confirmation by the terms of

the act of admission of the Territory or State into the Union, the State then becoming a trustee for school purposes.

These grants of land were made from the public domain, and to States only which were known as public-land States. Twelve States from March 3, 1803, known as public-land States, received the allowance of the sixteenth section to August 17, 1848. (See table. page 228.)

THE THIRTY SIXTH SECTION.

In the act for the organization of the Territory of Oregon, August 14, 1848, Senator Stephen A. Douglas inserted an additional grant for school purposes of the thirty-sixth section in each township, with indemnity for all public-land States thereafter to be admitted, making the reservation for school purposes the sixteenth and thirty-sixth sections, of 1,280 acres in each township, of six miles square reserved in public-land States and Territories, and confirmed by grant in terms in the act of admission of such State or Territory into the Union.

From March 13, 1853, to June 30, 1880, seven States have been admitted into the Union having a grant of the sixteenth and thirty-sixth sections, and the same area has been reserved in eight Territories.

UNIVERSITIES.

July 23, 1787, Congress, in the "Powers to the Board of Treasury to contract for the sale of Western Territory," ordered—

That not more than two complete townships be given perpetually for the purpose of an university, to be laid off by the purchaser or purchasers as near the centre as may be, so that the same shall be of good land, to be applied to the intended object by the legislature of the State.

This related to lands now in the State of Ohio, in the Symmes and Ohio Company purchases. They inaugurated the present method of taking from the public lands, for the support of seminaries of schools of a higher grade, the quantity of two townships at least, and in some instances more, to each of the States containing public lands, and special grants have also been made to private enterprises.

In the legislation relating to the admission of the public-land States into the Union, from the admission of Ohio in 1802 to the admission in 1876, grants of two townships of public-lands, viz, 46,080 acres each, for university purposes are enumerated. Ohio, Florida, Wisconsin and Minnesota are the exceptions, each having more than two townships in area. Nineteen States have had the benefit of this provision, and the two townships are reserved in the Territories of Washington, New Mexico and Utah. These will be granted and confirmed to them upon their admission into the Union. These reservations in each case require a special act. All school, university or agricultural college lands granted are sold by the legislature of the several States, or leased, and the proceeds of sale or lease applied to education.

MANNER OF SELECTING SCHOOL LANDS.

As soon as the running the lines of the public surveys, in school sections "in place" 16 and 36 are fixed and determined, the appropriation thereof for the educational object is, under the law, complete, and lists are made out and patents issued to the States therefor.

When sections 16 and 36 are found to be covered with prior adverse rights, such as legal occupancy and settlement by individuals under settlement laws, prior to survey of the lands, or deficient in area, because of fractional character of the townships, or from other causes, selections for indemnity are made.

INDEMNITY SELECTIONS.

Selections from other public lands as indemnity for deficiences in sections 16 and 36 and fractional townships under acts of May 20, 1826, and February 26, 1859, are made by agents appointed by the respective States, which selections are filed in the local offices of the district in which the land is situated, and if found to be correct, are certified to the General Land Office by the register of the local office where filed. If, upon examination by the Commissioner, the same are found to inure to the State, a list is made out and certified to the Secretary of the Interior for his approval. When approved, a certified copy of the same is transmitted to the Governor of the State in which the selections are made, and a copy thereof transmitted to the local office from which the selections are received, to be placed on file, and the approvals to be noted on its records.

By the approval of the Secretary, the fee is passed to the State. [See section 2449, Revised Statutes.]

The same course is pursued in making selections under the grants for internal improvements and agricultural colleges.

ACREAGE OF SIXTEENTH AND THIRTY-SIXTH SECTIONS.

The following statement shows the number of acres [estimated] to be embraced in the grant of Sections 16 in Louisiana for school purposes. Donaldson's Public Domain, pp. 223, 228.

STATEMENT OF THE GRANTS TO LOUISIANA FOR SCHOOL PURPOSES.

Louisiana, 786,044 acres, April 21, 1806; February 15, 1843.

This historical data is correct to December 1st, 1883; also the statement of lands donated to Louisiana for schools.

ACT NO. 321 APPROVED MARCH 15, 1855. SEC. 31.

ART. CVIII.—FREE SCHOOL FUND.

The proceeds from the sale of lands donated by the United States to this State for the use and support of schools, except proceeds from the sale of the 16th Section in the various townships of the State specially donated by Congress to the schools in the respective townships, and the proceeds of all lands to the State after the 15th of March, 1855, and not specially granted for purposes other than for the public schools, which may hereafter be disposed of by the State, and the ten per cent net proceeds of the estate of deceased persons to which the State has or may become entitled by law, shall be held by the State as a loan and shall be and remain a perpetual fund to be called the Free School Fund, on which the State shall pay an annual interest of six per cent., which interest, together with the interest of the trust fund deposited with this State by the United States, under the act of Congress approved the 23d of June, 1836, with the rents of all unsold lands, except that of the 16th Section, shall be appropriated for the support of public schools in this State; and donations of all kinds which shall be made for the support of schools and such other means as the legislature may from time to time set apart for school purposes, shall form part of the fund, and shall be also a loan on which the State shall pay an interest of six per cent *per annum.*

The Treasurer of the State is ordered to apply annually and to receive from the general government the said ten per cent of moneys now due and to become due to this State and to place the same when received to the credit of the proper fund, and to report thereon at each session of the General Assembly.

´ ACT 182, APPROVED MARCH 19, 1857.

ART. CIX.— PERPETUAL AND TRUST FUND TO BEAR SIX PER
CENT INTEREST PER ANNUM.

SEC. 1 of said act made it the duty of the Auditor and the State Treasurer, under the direction of the Governor, to ascertain the amount due by the State, on the 1st of July, 1857.

ART. CX.— BONDS.

SEC. 2.   Bonds were issued payable in forty years, bearing six per cent interest *per annum* for the amount ascertained to be due to the Free School Fund and the Seminary Fund.

ART. CXI.—INTEREST.

SEC. 3.   The said interest was to be paid *from the general fund.*

ART. CXII.—ACCUMULATIONS AND REINVESTMENTS.

SEC. 4.   The 183 bonds remaining in the redemption of the State Debt Fund, after the withdrawal of the 78 bonds, for the payment of which said fund was partially created, as appeared by the account of said debt on the 1st of January, 1857, together with the annual accumulations and re-investments, shall remain as a special trust fund which shall never be used for any other purpose than that for which it was and is pledged.

ART. CXIII.— RENT OF 16TH SECTION TO BE PAID TO PARISH TREASURERS.

SEC. 10 of act 182, of the year 1857, provides that the rents of the 16th Section shall not be paid in the State Treasury, but shall be paid to the Parish Treasurer, and shall be subject to the orders of the school directors of the district.

ART. CXIV.— TRUST FUND.

SEC. 13 of this act, indeed. all laws provide for a perpetual and sacred Fund, and the interest fixed upon the capital was six per cent.

The proceeds of all lands heretofore granted by the United States for the use and support of free schools and of all other property, shall be and remain a perpetual fund on which the State shall pay an annual interest of six per cent * * * and this appropriation shall remain inviolable. Constitution of 1868, Art. 139.

ACT NO. 81, APPROVED MAY 25, 1872.

ART. CXV.— ABOLISHMENT OF THE SCHOOL FUND.

SEC. 3 of said act reads: The fund in the State Treasury created by act No. 182, approved March 19, 1857, known as the free school fund, be and the same is hereby abolished, and in lieu thereof it is hereby made the duty of the auditor of public accounts to ascertain annually the aggregate amount which would be due the several parishes from the free school fund, if it were retained in the form in which it was prior to the passage of this Act, and to levy and collect a special tax to provide for the payment of the same to the several parishes when due, the same as if the free school fund had not been abolished. All moneys, bonds, and other assets belonging to said free school fund, in the State Treasury at the time this Act goes into effect, shall be transferred by the State Treasurer to the credit of the special fund created in the second section of this Act.

NOTA.—This was an act of outrageous spoliation and was denounced as such by the Supreme Court. Sun Mutual Ins. Co. vs. Board of Liquidation. 31 Ann. 175.

Act 81 violates the faith and solemn pledges of the State and the obligation is one the State is not at liberty to abolish. Ex rel. Durant. 29 Ann. 77.

CONSTITUTION OF THE YEAR 1879.

ART. CXVI — FREE SCHOOL FUND, SEMINARY FUND AND AGRICLUTURAL AND MECHANICAL COLLEGE FUND.

The debt due by the State to the free school fund is hereby declared to be the sum of one million, one hundred and thirty thousand, eight hundred and sixty - seven dollars and fifty - one cents in principal, and shall be placed on the books of the Auditor and Treasurer to the credit of the several townships entitled to the same; the said principal being the proceeds of the sales of lands heretofore granted by the United States for the use and support of free schools, which amount shall be held as a loan and shall be and remain a perpetual fund, on which the State shall pay an annual interest of four per cent from the 1st day of January, 1880; and that said interest shall be paid to the several townships in the State entitled to the same in accordance with the act of Congress No. 68, approved February 15, 1843; and the bonds of the State heretofore issued, under act of the General Assembly No. 81 of 1872, are declared null and void. Constitution of the year 1879, Art. 233.

The payment of interest on the Seminary Fund is fixed at four per cent on the amount of $136,000. The payment of interest on the Agricultural and Mechanical College is fixed on the amount of $182,313 03 at five per cent.

NOTA.—The State was previously pledged to the payment of six per cent. on these amounts out of the general fund, but under Act 233 of the Constitution, the interest provided for shall be paid out of any tax that may be levied and collected for the general purposes of public education, and is now reduced to four per cent., although the State Constitution of 1868 provided for the payment of six per cent.

An amount is levied annually for the maintenance of the free public schools.

A part of this amount is applied to the payment of the State's indebtedness.

The amount is twice applied to the maintenance of the schools.

First. In the General Revenue, Act 85, of 1888, Sec. 89, providing that $1\frac{1}{8}$ mill shall be levied for the free public schools.

Second. Under this article of the Constitution sufficient is taken for the payment of this interest out of the amount already appropriated for the maintenance of the schools.

Those acts, now repealed, act 182, of the year 1857, and act 321, of 1855, Sec. 31, were equitable and just in providing for the payment of this interest from the General Fund.

This is all final. *Un fait accompli.* But it may be that hereafter the legislator will readily favor the adoption of laws increasing the amounts necessary for the proper maintenance of the free public schools when he is reminded that the capital fixed is not as large as it should be and that the interest has been considerably reduced, despite the pledge of the State, and when it further occurs to him that an amount already appropriated for the maintenance of the schools is applied to the payment of the interest due to the schools.

ART. CXVII.—TAXATION POSSIBLE TO ERECT AND CONSTRUCT PUBLIC BUILDINGS.

Article 209, of the constitution of 1879, authorizes the increase of taxation on certain conditions, "for the purpose of erecting and constructing public buildings, bridges and works of public improvements in parishes, when the rate of such increase and the purpose for which it is intended, shall have been submitted to a vote of the property tax payers of such parish, entitled to a vote under the election laws of the State, and a majority of same voting at such election shall have voted therefor."

ACT 126 OF 1882.

IMPROVEMENT TAX.

ART. CXVIII.—"Act 126, and not Act 41, of 1882, is the law intended by the legislature to make effective Article 209." Duperier vs. Viator et als., 35 Aun. 960.

ART. 209. The State tax on property for all purposes whatever; including expenses of government, schools, levees and interest shall not exceed in any one year six mills on the dollar of its assessed valuation, if the ordinance regarding the bonded debt of the State is adopted and ratified by the people; and if said ordinance is not adopted and ratified by the people, said State tax for all purposes aforesaid shall not exceed in any one year five mills on the dollar on the assessed valuation of the property; and no parish or municipal tax for all purposes whatsoever shall exceed ten mills on the dollar of valuation; provided, that for the purpose of erecting and constructing public buildings, bridges and works of public improvement in parishes and municipalities, the rates of taxation herein limited may be increased when the rate of such increase, and the purpose for which it is intended, shall have been submitted to a vote of the property tax payers of such parish of municipality entitled to a vote under the election laws of the State, and a majority of same voting at such election shall have voted therefor.

LAW TO MAKE EFFECTIVE ART 209, OF THE CONSTITUTION OF 1879.

ACT 126, OF THE YEAR 1882.

ART. CXIX.—SPECIAL TAX. HOW LEVIED.

SEC. 1. That whenever one-tenth of the property tax payers

of any parish, city, incorporated town or municipality in this State shall petition the police jury, city, town or municipal authorities to levy an increased rate of taxation for the purpose of constructing public buildings, bridges without draws and works of public improvements in such parish, city, town or municipality, the said police jury, city, town or municipal authorities shall order a special election for that purpose, and shall submit to a vote of the property tax payers of such parish, city, town or municipality entitled to vote under the election laws of the State, the rate of taxation and the purpose for which it is intended: *provided*, that said election be held under the general election laws of the State at that time in force, and at the polling places at which the last preceding general election was held, and not sooner than twenty days after the official publication of the petition and ordinance ordering the election, which shall be made in the same manner provided by law for judicial advertisement.

ART. CXX.—DECISION.

" The vote of the majority of the property tax payers who voted at the election ordered * * * was therefore sufficient to carry the election." Duperier vs. Viator, 35 Ann. 960.

ART. CXXI.—PUBLICATION.

SEC. 3. The publication of the result of said election shall be made by ten days advertisement immediately thereafter, and the police juries, city, town and municipal authorities shall have the same power to enforce the collection of any special tax that may be authorized by said election as by law provided for the collection of other taxes.

ART. CXXII.—SCHOOL HOUSE AND PUBLIC IMPROVEMENT.

The law authorizes the levy of a special tax for the erection of public buildings and other improvements.

A school house is a public building for the free public schools, and it certainly is a public improvement.

POWER OF THE DISTRICT BOARD OF SCHOOL DIRECTORS WITH REFERENCE TO EXPROPRIATIONS.

SEC. 1298 When land shall be required for the erection of a school house, or for enlarging a school house lot, and the owner refuses to sell the same for a reasonable compensation, the District Board of School Directors shall have the power to select and possess such sites embracing space sufficiently extensive to answer the purpose of school house and grounds.

RELATIVE TO THE VALUE OF THE GROUNDS.

SEC 1299. Should such land holder deem the sum assessed too small, he shall have the right to institute suit before any proper judicial tribunal for his claim; but the title shall pass from him to the school corporation.

FAILURE OF OFFICERS TO PERFORM DUTY IMPOSED.

SEC. 1300. R. S. A failure on the part of any district, parish or State officer to perform the duty imposed upon him by any section of this act, under the title " Education," and in the manner herein specified, is hereby declared a misdemeanor in office Upon conviction thereof, such officer shall be punished by a fine not less than fifty, and not exceeding one hundred dollars, and by imprisonment in the parish prison for a term of not less than thirty days, and not exceeding three months. All prosecutions for offenses against this section shall have precedence over all cases before any justice of the peace, parish or district Court.

THE SALE WHICH CAN BE MADE BY THE REGISTER OF THE LAND OFFICE.

SEC. 1305 R. S. It shall be lawful for the Register of the Land Office to sell, at the price stipulated by law, to any Board of Free School Directors of this State, any amount, not less than five acres, of any land within their school district, donated by Congress to this State, either for the use of a Seminary of learning, or for the purpose of internal improvement on which to erect a school house.

HOW LOCATED.

SEC. 1306. Any land so sold shall commence in the corner of a legal division or sub-divisions of sections; and if in a right angle, it shall be run an equal distance on two sides, bounded by the line of such division, and form a square including the number of acres sold; if in an acute angle, it shall be bounded by said division lines to such distance, and by lines in such other directions as the Register may deem most equitable between the land so sold and that retained; the patents for lands so sold shall issue to the free school directors and their successors, for the use of their district schools, setting forth the number, and of what parish.

RESERVATIONS OF SCHOOL LANDS.

SEC. 1307. The Register of the State Land Office at Baton Rouge is required to ascertain in what township in this State, there are no reservations of school sections by reason of conflicting claims or from any other cause, or where the reservation is less than contemplated by law; and in such cases it is made his duty, under the superintendence of the Governor, to apply for, and as soon as possible, obtain a location of any land or part of land in lieu thereof.

SCRIPS SHOULD ISSUE ONLY WHEN LOCATIONS CANNOT BE MADE.

SEC. 1308. When such locations cannot be made, if deemed more advantageous to the State, the Register, with the assent of the Federal Government, is authorized to issue scrip for such lands, which scrip shall not be sold for a less amount than one dollar and twenty-five cents per acre.

FREE SCHOOL FUND.

SEC. 1313. The proceeds of all lands heretofore granted by the United States to this State for the use or support of schools, except the sixteenth section in the various townships of the States specially reserved by Congress for the use and benefit of the people therein; and all lands which may hereafter be granted or bequeathed to the State, and not specially granted or bequeathed for any other purpose, which hereafter may be disposed of by the State, and the ten per cent of the net proceeds of the sales of the public land which have accrued and are to accrue to this State under the act of Congress, entitled " An Act to appropriate the proceeds of the public lands," and to grant pre-emption rights, approved September 4, 1841; and the proceeds of the estates of deceased persons, to which the State has or may become entitled by law, shall be held by the State as a loan, and shall be and remain a perpetual fund, to be called the Free School Fund, on which the State shall pay an annual interest of six per cent; which interest, together with the interest of the Trust Fund deposited with this State by the United States, under the act of Congress approved the 23d of June, 1836, with the rents of all unsold lands, except that of the sixteenth sections, shall be appropriated for the support of public schools in this State; and donations of all kinds which shall be made for the support of schools, and such other means which the Legislature may from time to time set apart for school purposes, shall form a part of the fund, and shall also be a loan on which the State shall pay an interest of six per cent per annum.

It shall be the duty of the Treasurer of the State to apply annually, and to receive from the General Government, the said ten per cent of moneys now due and to become due to this State, and to place the same, when received, to the credit of the proper fund, and to report thereon to each session of the General Assembly.

REVISED STATUTES RELATIVE TO THE SALE OF SCHOOL LANDS.

ART. CXXIII. — SCHOOL LANDS.   THEIR SALES.   HOW TO BE MADE.   DUTY OF PARISH TREASURER RESPECTING PUBLIC SCHOOL LANDS.

SEC. 2958.   It shall be the duty of the parish treasurers of the several parishes in this State to have taken the sense of the inhabitants of the township, to which they may belong, any lands heretofore reserved and appropriated by Congress for the use of schools, whether or not the same shall be sold, and the proceeds invested as authorized by an Act of Congress approved February 15, 1843.   Polls shall be opened and held in each township, after advertisement, for thirty days at three of the most public places in the Town, and at the Court House door, and the sense of the legal voters therein shall be taken within the usual hours, and in the usual manner of holding elections, which elections shall be held and votes received by a member of the parish school board or a justice of the peace; and if a majority of the legal voters be in favor of selling the school lands therein, the same may be sold, but not otherwise.   The result of all such elections shall be transmitted to the parish treasurer, and by him to the State Superintendent.

ART. CXXIV. — SURVEY OF SCHOOL LANDS.

SEC. 2959.   Before making sale of the school lands belonging to the State, it shall be the duty of the parish treasurer, or other persons whose duty it may become to superintend the sales, to cause a re-survey of such lines as from any cause may have become obliterated or uncertain; and for this purpose he is authorized to employ the parish surveyor, or on his default, any competent surveyor; and the lines thus surveyed shall be marked in such manner as to enable those interested to make a thorough examination before sale, and all advertisements made for the sale of such lands shall contain a full description thereof according to the original survey and that required by this section.   The expenses of the survey shall be paid by the Auditor of Public Accounts out of the proceeds of the sale of the lands on the warrants of the parish treasurer.

ART. CXXV. — SALE ON THE ORDER OF THE AUDITOR.

SEC. 2960.   If the majority of the votes taken in a township shall give their assent to the sale of the lands aforesaid, the parish treasurer shall forthwith notify the Auditor of Public Accounts of the vote thus taken, and upon his order, the said lands shall be sold by the parish treasurer, at public auction, before the Court house door, by the sheriff or an auctioneer to be employed by the treasurer at his expense, to the highest bidder, in quantities not

less than 40 acres, nor more than 160, after having been previously
appraised by three sworn appraisers, selected by the parish treasurer and recorder of the parish, after (30) thirty days advertisement, but in no case at a less sum than the appraised value, payable on a credit of ten years as follows: ten per cent in cash and
the balance in nine annual installments, the interest to be paid
on the whole amount, annually, at the rate of eight per cent *per
annum*; the notes shall be made payable to the Auditor of Public
Accounts, secured by special mortgage on the land sold, and personal security *in solido*, until final payment of principal and interest; in the event of the purchaser neglecting or refusing to pay
any of these installments or interest at maturity, the mortgage
shall be forthwith closed, and the parish treasurer is hereby authorized to advertise and sell the land as before provided for, and
further authorized and required to execute all acts of sale on behalf of the State for any such lands sold, to receive the cash payment and notes given for the purchase, which shall be made payable to the State treasurer, and to place the same in the office of
the Auditor of Public Accounts, for collection; all cash received,
either for principal or interest, from said sales shall be transmitted by him to the State Treasurer, and any moneys thus
received into the State treasury from sales aforesaid shall bear
interest at the rate of six per cent *per annum*, and be credited to
the township to which the same belongs according to the provisions of the act of Congress. The parish treasurer shall forthwith notify the State Superintendent of the result of all sales
made by him. The parish treasurer shall be authorized to receive the whole amount bid for the lands, deducting the eight per
cent interest which the credits will bear.

ART. CXXVI.—SALE OF SECTIONS, DIVIDED BY LINES OF PAR-
ISHES.

SEC. 2966. When the 16th section of any township is divided
by a parish line, the treasurer of the parish in which a greater
portion of the section may lie, shall proceed to take the sense of
the people of the township, and to sell the same as provided by
law, as if the whole section lay in his parish; *provided*, that the
sale shall be advertised at the courthouses of both parishes.

ART. CXXVII.—TREASURER'S COMMISSION.

SEC. 2660. The parish treasurers of the several parishes shall
be entitled to retain out of the proceeds of the sale of 16th sections effected by them a percentage of $2\frac{1}{2}$ on the amount of said
sales, to be deducted from the cash payment, and the same shall
be in full compensation of their services.

ART. CXXVIII.—LEASE OF SCHOOL LANDS

SEC. 2962. Should a majority of the legal votes be against the
sale of the lands, then it shall be the duty of the parish board of
directors, where the same may be situated, to secure them from

injury and waste, and prevent illegal possession or aggression of any kind, and in conjunction with the parish treasurer to lease the same, or any part thereof, for a term not exceeding four years, according to the provisions of the second section of the Act of Congress aforesaid, and to inform the State Superintendent thereof.

ART. CXXIX.—PROCEEDS OF LANDS ACCRUING TO TOWNSHIPS.

SEC. 2963. All moneys that have been or may be hereafter received into the State Treasury, and the interest that has or may accrue thereon from the sale of any 16th section of school lands or the school land warrants belonging to the various townships in the State, shall be placed to the credit of the township, and should the people of any township desire to receive for the use of the schools therein, the annual interest payable by the State on funds deposited to their credit, or the annual proceeds of the loan, the parish treasurer shall, on the petition of five legal voters in any such township, order an election to be held in the township, as provided for the sale of township lands; and if a majority of any number of votes above seven be in favor of receiving annually the accruing interest as aforesaid, the same shall be paid to the treasurer of the parish for the use of the townships or districts; otherwise the interest shall be an accumulated fund to their credit until so called for.

ART. CXXX.—MODE OF ANNULLING SALES.

SEC. 2965. In all cases of the sale of the school lands known as 16th sections, heretofore made, where the purchase money has not been paid, the purchaser or purchasers shall have the right to annul the sale upon application to the District Court of the parish where the land is situated; provided, that the judgment of nullity shall be obtained at the cost of the applicant and contradictorily with the District Attorney, in conjunction with the school directors of the district in which said land is situated, who shall be made a party defendant in such suit; provided also, that it shall appear upon the hearing that the value of the land has not been impaired by any act of the purchaser; and provided further, that nothing in this act shall be so construed as to entitle the said purchaser to repayment of any part of the purchase money already paid.

No. 57. To provide for the collection of notes given for the purchase price of sixteenth sections, known as Free School Lands.

DUTY OF AUDITOR IN PROVIDING FOR THE COLLECTION OF NOTES GIVEN IN PAYMENT OF THE SIXTEENTH SECTIONS.

SEC. 1. Be it enacted by the General Assembly of the State of Louisiana, That it shall be the duty of the Auditor of Public

Accounts, immediately on the passage of this act, to forward for collection to the Treasurer of the School Board in their respective parishes throughout the State, all the notes given for the purchase price of sixteenth sections, or any part thereof, known as free school lands, whenever any installment of said purchase price has become due or may become due, and it shall be the duty of said Treasurer of Parish School Board to receive and receipt for same.

DUTY OF PARISH TREASURER IN COLLECTING SAID NOTES—

PROVISO.

SEC. 2. Be it further enacted, etc , That it shall be the duty of the Treasurer of the Parish School Board, on receipt of the notes due and given for the said sixteenth sections, to immediately notify the principal and his sureties, in writing, of the amount of said note, principal and interest, due and unpaid ; provided, said lands for which said notes were given are still in possession of the original purchaser, and if in the possession of other parties, such possessor shall also be likewise notified of all the demands, principal and interest, against said lands, and if all the demands against the same be not satisfied within thirty days from said notice, it shall be the duty of the Treasurer of the Parish School Board to turn over said notes to the District Attorney for said district, or other attorney selected by the School Board, for suit ; and, provided further, that said notice shall serve as a bar to prescription, which shall only begin to run from the service of said notice.

DUTY OF DISTRICT ATTORNEY OR OTHER ATTORNEY SELECTED

BY SCHOOL BOARD TO COLLECT SAID NOTES--

MODE OF PROCEEDING IN SUCH

COLLECTION.

SEC. 3. Be it further enacted, etc., That it shall be the duty of the said attorney to proceed without delay, by all necessary legal processes, and without depositing clerk's or sheriff's costs, or giving security therefor, to collect all such notes as may be turned over to him by said Treasurer of the Parish School Board, and given for sixteenth sections, known as free school lands, and if any of the conservatory writs should be found to be necessary in order to aid in said collection, it shall be lawful to issue the same, without giving bond as required in other cases.

COMPENSATION TO SAID ATTORNEY FOR COLLECTING SAID NOTES
—DUTY OF THE ATTORNEY UPON COLLECTING SAID
NOTES—HOW HE SHALL APPLY THE SAME—
DUTY OF PARISH TREASURER IN
RELATION THERETO—WHAT
DISPOSITION SHALL BE
MADE OF SUCH
MONEYS.

SEC. 4. Be it further enacted, etc., That the said attorney shall receive ten per cent of all money collected by him on notes given for sixteenth sections, and after deducting said ten per cent he shall turn over the remainder to the Treasurer of the School Funds for the parish in which said lands are situated, and the same shall be transmitted through the Auditor of Accounts, by said treasurer, to the State Treasurer; and any moneys thus received into the State Treasury from said collections shall bear interest at the rate of four per cent per annum, and be credited to the township to which the same belongs, according to the provisions of the Act of Congress.

SEC. 5. Be it further enacted, etc.. That all laws or parts of laws in conflict herewith be and the same are hereby repealed.

ART. CXXXI.—CAPITAL DUE THE SEVERAL TOWNSHIPS.

By joint resolution of 1886, the Auditor is authorized to fix the amount of capital due the several townships from the sales of sixteenth sections school lands, made since January 1st, 1880, and to warrant for interest due thereon.

ART. CXXXII.—AUDITOR TO ASCERTAIN AMOUNTS DUE TOWN- SHIPS.

As there has been paid into the State Treasury from the sale of sixteenth sections school lands, made since January 1st, 1880, a large sum of money over which Article 233 of the Constitution has no control, and the same having been invested in Louisiana four per cent bonds, as required by the Act of Congress, approved February 15, 1843, and Act No. 265 of 1855 of the General Assembly of Louisiana, and the interest on said bonds having been collected by the State Treasurer and now at the credit of the several townships, it shall be the duty of the Auditor of Public Accounts, by the first day of January, 1887, to ascertain the amount of capital that may be due the several townships from the proceeds of the sales of sixteenth sections Vide Act of Congress of the 26th September, approved 15th February, 1843, Statutes at Large, Vol. 5, p. 600.

ART. CXXXIII.—CURRENT FUNDS FOR SCHOOLS IN STATE
TREASURY.

SEC. 1326. An account shall be opened on the books of the Treasurer; in this account shall be charged the annual expenditures of the public schools and credited with the net receipts for the special taxes laid by the General Assembly for the public schools.

It is made the Auditor's duty to present a statement of the condition of this fund in his annual report, and an estimate of the special tax needed for the support of the public schools during the ensuing year, beyond the receipts for said support from other sources.

It is made the duty of the Superintendent to furnish the Auditor with all the information he may require for his said report.

JOINT RESOLUTION No. 96, APPROVED JULY 8, 1886.

ART. CXXXIV. – CAPITAL DUE THE SEVERAL TOWNSHIPS.

The Auditor is authorized to fix the amount of capital due the several townships from the sales of sixteenth sections school lands made since January 1st, 1880, and to issue warrant for the interest due thereon.

The Auditor is directed to ascertain the amount of capital that may be due the several townships from the proceeds of the sales of sixteenth sections, made since the first of January, 1880, and actually paid in the State Treasury

The amount ascertained shall be the capital upon which interest shall be thereafter allowed, and paid out of the interest collected on the bonds to the township, the sixteenth section of which have been sold since January 1st, 1880. No interest to be allowed for fractions of the year, but it shall commence on the first of January of the year after receipt.

The interest due upon the capital ascertained as aforesaid, and the interest due upon subsequent sales, shall be paid to the townships in the manner provided. It shall be the duty of the Auditor to furnish the Treasurer and Superintendent of Public Education with a statement of the amount due each township.

ACT No. 14, ADOPTED JUNE 16, 1882.

TRESPASS ON SIXTEENTH SECTION.

To prevent trespass on free school lands known as sixteenth sections, and to prescribe penalties for a violation of the provisions of this act.

ART. CXXXV.—TIMBER ON SIXTEENTH SECTIONS—CUTTING OR BURNING SAME.

That whoever shall cut down, or remove for sale for his own use, or the use of another, any timber on any free school land in this State, belonging to the State, known as sixteenth sections, shall be deemed guilty of a misdemeanor, and upon conviction shall be condemned to pay a fine of not less than fifty nor more than one thousand dollars, and in default of the same, be sentenced to imprisonment not less than ten days nor more than one year.

ART. CXXXVI.—CULTIVATION OR INCLOSING SIXTEENTH SECTIONS—PENALTIES.

SEC. 2. That whoever shall knowingly use, cultivate or inclose any free school land, known as the sixteenth section, without authority from the parish board of school directors, shall on conviction be condemned to pay a fine of not less than fifty nor more than one thousand dollars, and in default of the same be sentenced to imprisonment for not less than ten days nor more than one year.

SECTION 1320, REVISED STATUTES

ART. CXXXVII.—SCHOOL PROPERTY EXEMPT FROM SEIZURE.

Property dedicated to the use, and belonging to public schools, or employed by municipal corporations for the purpose, shall be exempt from seizure.

Article 207 of 1879 was amended by joint resolution, 92, of the regular session of 1886, No. 6 of the amendments, submitted to the vote of the people at the general election held April, 1888. Property used for colleges or other school purposes are exempt vide, also Tulane vs. Board of Assessors, 38 A. 297.

ART. CXXXVIII.—SIXTEENTH SECTIONS, AND COURT DECISIONS RESPECTING THEM.

Under the general laws, and where the township is surveyed in square sections, every sixteenth section is reserved as school land, in fractional or irregular townships on water courses, the Secretary of the Treasury is required by law to select and designate the school lands.

Board vs. Rollins, 33 A. 424.
Bres. vs. Louviere, 37 A. 736.

By issuing an indemnity school warrant the State parts with what title in the public domain it could by location have secured. The divestiture is complete when the location is approved, and on return and surrender the Governor issues a patent.

NOTA.—Whenever the township is not surveyed in square sections, but is a fractional or irregular township on a water course or for other cause is fractional or irregular, the school authorities should see that the selection is legal, or that proper selection and location be made.

ART. CXXXIX.—ILLEGAL CERTIFICATES OF INDEBTEDNESS.

" Certificates of indebtedness, issued by the Board of School Directors of the public schools for services rendered in 1874, are not binding upon the City of New Orleans " [Labat vs. New Orleans, 38th Ann., 283.]

ART. CXL.—DISCHARGE OF AN OFFICER

" To obtain his discharge, an officer should obtain a clear receipt from the board of school directors, in so far as he has incurred any responsibility as an officer in which the said board is concerned." [33d Ann , 709; State ex rel vs. Sheriff.]

SCHOOL LANDS.

" The minimum price of school lands is one dollar and a quarter per acre." [School Directors vs. Coleman, 14th Ann., 186.]

ART. CXLI.—SALES OF SIXTEENTH SECTIONS.

It is of importance to establish what sales have been made of the sixteenth sections.

What payments have been made.

What sales have been cancelled, that the State officer may direct the collection of unpaid notes, representing the purchase price of these sections sold, and that the whole of the amount appropriated for the payment of interest on the school fun l, viz: the sum of $45,234 70, for the year ending June, 1889, and a similar amount for the year ending June, 1890, may be properly credited to the townships.

This depends upon the different school boards, who should not fail to take proper steps to properly establish the amount to which each township is entitled.

PRESCRIPTION OF DEBTS DUE TO ANY CHARITABLE INSTITUTION OF THIS STATE, TO ANY COLLEGE FUND AND FUND OF ANY INSTITUTION OF LEARNING, OR TO ANY INSTITUTION OF LEARNING, OR TO ANY FUND BEQUEATHED FOR CHARITABLE PURPOSES, FOR DIS- TRIBUTION TO THE POOR, SHALL BE THIRTY YEARS.

No. 103. Relative to the prescription of debts due to certain charitable and educational institutions and funds.

Be it enacted by the General Assembly of the State of Louisiana, That the term of prescription of any and all debts, due to any charitable institution in this State, to any college fund, or fund of any institution of learning, or to any fund bequeathed for charitable purposes, for the purpose of distribution to the poor or indigent, or for purposes of education, and of all debts contracted by borrowing the whole or part of any such funds, shall be thirty years; provided, the debt is evidenced by writing.

HYGIENE AND TEMPERANCE.

ACT 40, APPROVED JULY 6, 1888.

TO PROVIDE FOR THE STUDY OF SCIENTIFIC TEMPERANCE OR OF THE NATURE OF ALCOHOLIC DRINKS AND NARCOTICS, AND THEIR EFFECTS UPON THE HUMAN SYSTEM, IN CON-
NECTION WITH THE SEVERAL DIVISIONS OF THE SUBJECT OF RELATIVE PHYSIOLO-
GY AND HYGIENE, BY THE PUPILS IN THE PUBLIC SCHOOLS IN LOUISIANA.

ART. CXLII.— INSTRUCTION TO BE GIVEN.

SECTION 1. That in addition to the branches, in which instruction is now given in the public schools, instruction shall also be given as to the nature of alcoholic drinks and narcotics, and special instruction as to their effects upon the human system in connection with the several divisions of the subject of relative physiology and hygiene, and such subjects shall be taught as regularly as other branches are taught in said schools. Such instruction shall be given orally from a text book in the hand of the teacher, to pupils who are not able to read, and shall be given by the use of text books in the hands of the pupils in the case of those who are able to read, and such instruction shall be given as aforesaid to all pupils in all public schools in the State, to all the grades until completed in the high schools.

ART. CXLIII.— TEXT BOOKS.

SEC. 2. That the text books used for the instruction required to be given by the preceding section, shall give at least one-fourth of their space to the consideration of the nature and effects of alcoholic drinks and narcotics; and the books used in the highest grades of graded schools shall contain at least twenty pages of matter relating to this subject.

Text books on physiology in use, in the schools or at the time this act takes effect, which are not in accordance with the requirements of this section, shall be changed for books satisfying the requirements of this section, except when previous contracts as to such text books now in force.

ART. CXLIV.—EXAMINATION OF TEACHERS ON THE SUBJECT.

SEC. 3. That no certificate shall be granted hereafter to any new applicant to teach in the public schools of Louisiana, who has not passed a satisfactory examination in the study of the nature of alcoholic drinks and narcotics, and of their effects upon the human system, in connection with the several divisions of the subject of relative physiology and hygiene.

ART. CXLV.— CERTIFICATE TO BE FILED BY THE TEACHER.

SEC. 4. That each teacher of any school in this State supported wholly or in part from public money, shall, before receiving any renumeration for services rendered in said capacity, file a certificate with the person by whom such payments are authorized to be made, to the effect that such teacher has faithfully complied with all the provisions of this act during the entire period for which such payment is sought and in the manner specified in this act, and no money shall be paid to any such teacher who has not filed such a certificate.

ART. CXLVI.—POSTPONEMENT IN SOME RESPECT OF THE EN-
FORCEMENT OF PART OF THE LAW.

SEC. 5. Section 3, referring to examinations of teachers and Section 4 to the payment of teachers will not take effect before October 1, 1890.

AN ACT—No. 126, APPROVED APRIL 10, 1880.

ART. CXLVII.— CERTIFICATES OF INDEBTEDNESS.

All valid certificates of indebtedness by the public school board of the City of New Orleans, and by all the parish school boards throughout the State, for the State's portion of the salaries of teachers and portresses and for the necessary expenses of conducting the public schools, prior to January 1, 1880, may be submitted to the Superintendent of Public Education for approval, and when approved said certificate may be presented to the Auditor of Public Accounts, who shall draw his warrant for the principal of said warrant on the State Treasurer, and shall distinctly state in each of said warrants that it is payable out of school and general fund taxes and licenses due the State of Louisiana, prior to January 1, 1880, and collected subsequently.

ART. CXLVIII.—WARRANTS ISSUED UNDER THE PRECEDING
SECTION.

These warrants may be presented to the Auditor of Public Accounts, State Treasurer and Attorney General, if valid they shall be endorsed as such and when they are surrendered to said officers and when they shall have been registered and cancelled, they shall issue to the holders certificates in sums of $5, $10, $20 or $50, as may be desired by the holder, which shall be receivable for all taxes and licenses due the State, subsequent to January 1, 1879, and prior to January 1, 1880, except taxes due, the interest and levee funds.

ART. CXLIX.—PROVISION—FURTHER UPON THE SUBJECT.

SEC. 3. That after all the certificates are retired which the Auditor, Treasurer and Attorney General, shall have issued for said Auditor's warrants, outstanding January 1st, 1880, in accordance with the constitutional ordinance for the relief of delinquent taxpayers, and after a sum of money from the collectors of delinquent taxes and licenses due the State prior to January 1st, 1879, shall have been set aside to pay the principal and interest of the five dollar bonds issued in accordance with said ordinance, the certificates provided by section 2, of this act shall be received for all taxes and licenses due the State prior to January 1st, 1879, and for all interest, penalties, fees and charges thereon, except taxes due the interest and levee funds.

ART. CL.—NOTICE TO BE ISSUED BY THE AUDITOR.

SEC. 4. That as soon as all the certificates are retired, and all five dollar bonds are fully provided for, as set forth in section 3, of this act, the Auditor of Public Accounts shall immediately issue his notice of that fact to each Tax Collector and Sheriff throughout the State; and, thereupon, said certificates issued under section 2, of this act, shall be received for all taxes and licenses due the State prior to January 1st, 1879, and for all interest, penalties, costs, fees and charges, except taxes due the interest and levee funds and may be tendered in payment of so much of the purchase price of all property purchased by or forfeited to the State, and sold in accordance with the act of the General Assembly providing for the sale of said property, as represent the taxes due the school and general funds, interest, penalties, costs, fees and charges thereon.

DISCIPLINE AND QUESTIONS IN THAT CONNECTION.

CIVIL CODE.

ART. CLI.—LEGAL AUTHORITIES ON THE SUBJECT OF SCHOOL DISCIPLINE.

Fathers and mothers may, during their life, delegate a part of their authority to teachers, school masters and others to whom they entrust their children for their education, such as the power of restraint and correction, so far as may be necessary to answer the purposes for which they employ them. Art. 220.

Judge Blackstone says " the master is in *loco parentis* and has such a portion of the powers of the parents committed to his charge as may be necessary to answer the purposes for which he is employed."

ART. CLII.—TEACHERS' JUDGMENT ABOUT DISCIPLINE.

SEC. 6. Relative to punishment, the calm and honest judgment of the teacher, as to the requirement, should have great weight in matters of discipline as in the case of a parent under similar circumstances. [American Law Register, Van Vacter vs. State; July number, 1888. *Discipline in School.*

It is the duty of a teacher to maintain proper discipline in school, and the extent of his authority in that direction is discussed. [Law Register, N. S. Vol. XIII, p. 716].

ART. CLIII.— BRANCHES OF STUDIES.

SEC. 7. Certain studies are required to be taught in the public schools by statute. The rights of one pupil must be so exercised undoubtedly as not to prejudice the equal rights of others.

Murrow vs. Wood, 13 American Law Register, p. 694.

NOTA.—The State Board has adopted certain studies to be taught in the free public schools. The local boards have the authority of carrying out the rules and regulations of the State Board. The studies are subject to their control, also all questions relating to grading the schools, and to the schools the pupils should attend when there are several schools in the same town or locality. In all this, however, due regard should be had for the wishes of the parents, but the parish board is the authority subject to such appeal as the law provides.

SEVERAL DECISIONS—NOTED IN THEIR GENERAL APPLICATION.

ART. CLIV.—SCHOOL DIRECTORS.

Are not authorized to bring suits for the revendication of land donated by Congress to the State for public school purposes, and sold under a law of the State.

School Directors vs. Ober, 32 Ann. 417.

SALE OF WARRANTS.

The treasurer of the State Board, may make a valid sale of the warrants of the State which represent the interest on the free school fund.

Board of Directors Concordia parish vs. Hernandez, 31 Ann. 158.

ILLEGAL CHARGES.

" The school board can not allow charges in violation of the law. Their action is *ultra*, and is not susceptible of ratifi-

cation.   Settlement made is not conclusive." [School Board ver-
sus Trimble, 33d Ann., 1073.]   '

RULES AND REGULATIONS.

" The various school boards and other educational authorities
of the State have, when the statutes are construed in connection
with the incidental powers, which the law gives all corporations,
the power to adopt rules and regulations for the schools under
their control." [Fertelle vs. Mischerer, 11 N. E., 605 (Indiana).

RECOVERY ON A BOND.

The school board's failure to require regular accounts and settlements from the Treasurer is not discharge of sureties.

Although the bond is made payable to the Governor of the
State, the President of the Board has the right to sue on the bond
executed by the Treasurer. [Board of School Directors and the
Parish of Madison vs. A. V. Brown and others, 33d Ann., 383.]

FIDUCIARY AND EX CONTRACTU—OBLIGATION.

"Action against agents and depositaries for damages caused by
their fraud or negligence or mis-management, is prescribed by
ten years." [7 R. 513, 3 L. 591.]

" The treasurer of the school board failing to account for funds
received by him in that capacity is bound ex contractu, and the
judgment is fiduciary in its character, and is only barred by the
prescription of ten years." [Board of School Directors vs. J. E.
Trimble, 32nd Ann. 793.]

SUITS BY THE SUPERINTENDENT OF PUBLIC EDUCATION.

" He has no authority to appear in person, nor to be represented by counsel of his own selection.   In any suit in which he
may be a party, he must be represented by the Attorney General or District Attorney."   [Fay vs. Burke, Treasurer, 35th
Ann. 369.]

PARISH SUPERINTENDENT.

" Charges by a county superintendent for official correspond-
ence, with teachers, school officers and others, all pertaining to
school affairs, and rendered in good faith, are proper items for
allowance." [Smith vs. County of Jefferson, Col. 13 p. 917].

OFFICERS—THEIR DUTIES AND RESPONSIBILITIES.

" A Treasurer of School Funds to whom the law prescribes a
mode of payment, can legally account for these funds only in

the manner provided." [Chas N. Ealer vs. Mills Spaugh, 32nd Ann., 901.]

TREASURER AND SURETIES.

"Principal and sureties are not protected by urging that the Treasurer has not taken the oath of office. It is presumed that he has taken the oath when he has discharged for some time the functions of his office.

"The sureties by signing the bond admitted the capacity of the principal."

DEFECTS OF FORM BY WAY OF SIGNING THE BOND.

"The rights of the sureties as against their principal not having been impaired, they cannot complain of his acts, his omission or commission." [School Directors vs. Judice and others, 39th Ann., 897.]

BOND—RECOURSE THEREON.

"The parish treasurer having defaulted, judgment is obtained against him, and the court holds a sagainst his sureties that the judgment against the principal is res adjudicata, as to the sureties, and within the limit of the amount for which they signed and obligated themselves as sureties. They are bound to make good the entire judgment against the principal, including the penalty.

"The sureties are liable for the five per cent per month penalty imposed upon a defaulting treasurer." [7th Ann., 131; 10th Ann., 492; 14th Ann., 679; Hazard Eastin et al vs. School Directors, 40th Ann., 706.]

TAXATION—EXEMPTION COMMERCIAL COLLEGE.

A commercial college is exempt from taxation under Article 207 of the Constitution. This exemption is not affected or impaired by the fact that the owner, who is the principal of the school, and one of the teachers, resides in the building. [Blackmar vs. Houston, tax collector, 39th Ann., 592.]

ONE OF THE POWERS OF THE SCHOOL COMMITTEE.

Committees have a legal right to refuse to examine a teacher as to literary qualifications if they are dissatisfied with his moral character. Case of Layton E. Seamens School Committee of Coventry.

PRIVILEGED COMMUNICATIONS.

A communication representing that a certain person was of bad moral character, and wholly unfit to teach and have the care of a school made to the proper authority for the sole purpose of preventing the issue to the person so charged of a license to teach school is held to be a privileged communication and not actionable. Wiman vs. Mabee, 45 Michigan 484.

An action will not lie on a communication relating to personal character, if made in good faith and for an honest purpose by persons concerned and to the proper person.

Nor will it lie when such a communication is untrue, if it is not maliciously made.

AN EXCERPT FROM BLACKSTONE.

The last duty of parents to their children is that of giving them an education, suitable to their situation in life; a duty pointed out by reason and of the greatest importance.

"For as Puffendorf well observed, it is not easy to imagine or allow that a parent has conferred any considerable benefit upon his child by bringing him into the world, if he afterwards entirely neglects to culture his education, and suffers him to grow up like a mere beast to lead a life useless to others and shameless to himself."

"Yet the municipal laws of most countries seem to be defective on this point, by not constraining the parent to bestow a proper education upon his children."

"Perhaps they thought it punishment enough to leave the parent, who neglected the instruction of his family, to labor under those griefs and inconveniences which his family so uninstructed will be sure to bring upon him."

Our laws, though their defects in this particular cannot be denied, have, in one instance, made wise provisions for bringing up the rising generation, since the poor and laboring part of the community, when pass the age of nurture, are taken out of the hands of their parents by the Statutes by apprenticing poor children, and are placed out by the people in such a manner as may render their abilities, in their several stations, of the greatest advantage to commonwealth.   Blackstone, book 1, page 451.

ART. CLV.--RATE OF COMPENSATION TO TEACHERS.

The compensation of teachers not being fixed by statute, they must be paid either according to their contract with the School Board or upon a *quantum meruit*.

Offut vs. Bourgeois, 13 Ann. 607.

THE EMPLOYMENT OF TEACHERS.

"The term of teachers for which employed limited to one year in New Orleans."   Golden vs. Board of School Directors, 34 Ann. 354.

DISCIPLINE.

Moderate restraint and correction of a pupil by his teacher is not an offense, but is authorized by law, and the authority of the teacher is not limited to the time the pupil is at the school room or under the actual control of the teacher. [Bolding vs. Texas, 4 S. W., 579.]

"The teacher is *loco parentis*, and authority is necessarily surrendered to him for proper government of the school." [Morrow vs. Wood, American Law Register, N. S. X. 3, 692.]

DAYS OF REST.

Section 11 of the Revised Statutes. "The following should be considered as days of public rest in this State, and no others, namely: The 1st of January; the 8th of January; the 22d of February; Mardi-Gras; 4th of March (in New Orleans); 4th of July; 25th of December; Sundays and Good Fridays."

ART. CLVI.—ERROR IN APPORTIONING SCHOOL FUNDS.

An error has been committed by the State Treasurer, on which the Superintendent of Public Education made an apportionment of funds. Before the apportionment could be canceled the School Board of Orleans had received their quota.

When a subsequent apportionment was made, the amount paid in error was deducted by the State Superintendent of Education.

On appeal, the Court confirmed the action of that officer.

State *ex rel.* vs. E. H. Fay, Supt., 36 Ann., 241.

ART. CLVII.—AMOUNTS PAID IN ERROR RECOVERABLE.

One School Board can stand in judgment against another, and recover funds erroneously paid by the State authorities. If the debtor Board has purchased property with the funds, the property itself can be secured in place of the funds which it represents. This section is not subject to the five years' prescription.

School Board vs. School Board, 36 Ann. 806.

NORMAL SCHOOLS.

ACT 51, APPROVED JULY 7TH 1884. ACT 61, APPROVED JULY 5TH, 1886. ACT 23, APPROVED JUNE 20TH. 1888.

ART CLVIII—NORMAL SCHOOLS AT NATCHITOCHES.

This school was established in accordance with the act of the Legislature No. 51, approved July 7, 1884. This act was amended by Act 61, of the year 1886, and Act 23 of the year 1888. The following is a compilation of the original Act and of the amendments.

ART. CLIX.—BOARD OF ADMINISTRATORS.

The appointment of the Board of Administrators devolves upon the State Board of Education.

ART. CLX.—RESIDENCE OF THE MEMBERS OF THE BOARD.

One member is appointed from each of the first four circuits of the Courts of Appeal and one member from the Town of Natchitoches. They are appointed for four years.

ART. CLXI.—AUTHORITY OF THE BOARD OF ADMINISTRATORS.

They elect the teachers.

Determine the salary each shall receive and they have charge of the affairs of the school and of the prosecution of its interests.

They are empowered to confer diplomas upon all graduates of the Normal School. This diploma entitles its holder to a State teacher's certificate which shall be valid for four years from its date.

ART. CLXII.—APPROPRIATIONS.

The appropriations are to be expended for the maintenance of the school and not for improvements.

ART. CLXIII.—ANNUAL SESSIONS.

The annual session commences on the first Monday and continues not less than seven months.

ART. CLXIV.—FACULTY.

The faculty consist of a President and such additional teachers as the interests of the school may require.

ART. CLXV.—COURSE OF STUDIES.

This shall include series of lectures upon the principles of education, the science and art of teaching, modes of discipline, school management and other branches with instructions on natural sciences, hygiene, physiology and such other branches of learning as the faculty with the approval of the Board of Administrators may elect.

The course of studies may be divided into three years, but there shall not be any preparatory departments.

ART. CLXVI.—CONDITIONS FOR ADMISSION.

To be admitted a student, must at least be sixteen years of age, of mental qualifications, white of either sex. The student must be proficient in the ordinary branches of common school education and must express a *bona fide* intention of teaching at least one year in the public schools of Louisiana after graduation.

ACT No. 124, APPROVED APRIL 30, 1877.

ART. CLXVII –SITE OF NORMAL SCHOOL IN NEW ORLEANS, UNDER CONTROL OF STATE BOARD OF EDUCATION.

SECTION 1.   The State Board of Education is authorized and directed to take possession and to assume the control of the site purchased for the State in September and October, 1860, for the location of the State Normal School, said site consisting of 4 lots in square 253, bounded by Baronne, Clio, Erato and Dryades streets, in the 1st Municipal District of New Orleans, and numbered 15, 16, 17 and 18, as more particularly described in the deed of sale executed before L. Ricardo, Notary Public, and duly recorded.

ART. CLXVIII. —STATE BOARD OF EDUCATION—RIGHT TO SELL.

SEC. 2.   The State Board of Education is authorized to appropriate said lots or the revenues or proceeds thereof towards the maintenance of said Normal school or schools as may be established by the city board of school directors in furtherance of the act to regulate public education, etc., passed by the General Assembly, and to this end the said Board may, in its discretion, rent out said lots or any portion thereof, to the City of New Orleans or any other purchaser, and convey a valid title therefor to the vendee on behalf of the State of Louisiana; provided, that the said lots or any portion thereof shall not be sold for less than was paid for the same; and *provided further*, that the revenues or proceeds of said lots shall be deposited with the City Treasurer, as treasurer of all school funds for the City of New Orleans, and shall be held by him as a special fund for the support of the Normal Schools, and be paid out by him only on warrants or checks drawn by the president and secretary of the city Board of School Directors in favor of the executive committee, or of the teachers in charge of the several school or schools under the control of said board; and *provided further*, that said city board shall make provisions for the gratuitous professional tuition and training in such Normal School or schools of at least one properly qualified student from each judicial district in this State.

ACT No. 143. APPROVED APRIL 15, 1880.

ART. CLXIX—TO AUTHORIZE THE STATEBOARD OF EDUCATION TO SELL CERTAIN PROPERTY,

SECTION 1. That the State Board of Education, or its legal successors, be and is hereby authorized and empowered to sell on such terms as it shall deem most favorable, any property now under its control, on such terms as it shall deem most favorable, any property now under its control, purchased for the use of State Normal Schools, on such terms as it shall deem most favorable, and to convey valid title therefor to the purchaser in the name and behalf of the State of Louisiana.

ART. CLXX.—PROCEEDS OF THE SALE—HOW TO BE APPRO-PRIATED.

SEC. 2. That the said State Board of Education, or its legal successors, is authorized to appropriate the proceeds of the sales of any property made under authority of section one of this act, and any rents derived from such property, to aid in the maintenance, during three or more years, of Normal Schools and departments in the State of Louisiana, for the purpose of enlarging the usefulness of said institutions, securing scholarships therein for advanced students, for the professional training of advanced students as teachers of the public schools, and for the scholastic improvement of any person, already teaching, who may desire and be able to attend such institutions, in the proportion of thirty dollars for each student so trained during at least seven months in the year, without charge for tuition ; *provided*, such Normal schools and departments be organized and conducted on such plan, and be subject to such rules and regulations as shall have been prescribed for their guidance by the State Board of Education or the State Superintendent of Public Education.

ART. CLXXI.—REPEALING CLAUSE.

SEC. 3. All conflicting laws are repealed.

ART. CLXXII.—NEW ORLEANS NORMAL SCHOOL.

The State Board of Education adopted, May 30, 1885, the following resolution, viz :

That the accumulated rents and revenues derived from the rental of the State Normal School property, situated in New Orleans be turned over to the Board of Directors of the Public Schools of New Orleans for the use of a Normal School, to be established in the city of New Orleans by the said Board ; provided, such Normal School be established on or before the first day of January, 1886, and provided further, that the plan of organization of such school should be submitted to the Board of Education for approval.

ART. CLXXIII.—PLAN OF ORGANIZATION OF THE NORMAL SCHOOL

1.—The school to be located in the Girls' High School building on Calliope street.

2.—Daily sessions to be held on at least three school days of the week, and on Saturday morning, during such hours as may be determined hereafter by the Board of Directors as most convenient and advantageous to the students.

3.—The annual session to be not less than six months, provide the means at the disposal of the directors are sufficient to pay teachers and defray other necessary expenses for that time.

4.—No student shall be admitted to the Normal Schools who is less than sixteen years of age; nor shall any student be admitted by transfer from grammar departments of our Public Schools, without an intervening course of studies.

5.—Admission and promotion from one class to a higher, shall be by regular examination. The design of the school will be to promote the preparation and qualification of teachers for their work, and to encourage a preliminary course of study such as is pursued in our Girls' High School and in other institutions of similar grade. Rules for admission and graduation of students must have reference to this end.

6.—The course of instruction in the various classes of the Normal School shall embrace:

a.—A review, from the teacher's standpoint, of the ordinary branches of a common school education.

b.—Physiology and hygiene, with the aid of any course of lectures which may be given to teachers, under the sanction of the Board, upon these subjects.

c.—Drawing.

d.—Theory and practice of teaching.

7.—Instruction free.

8.—The Normal school is under the management and control of the New Orleans Board of Directors. They select the teachers; pass all necessary regulations for the admission and graduation of students:

1.—The teachers are a principal and two assistants.

2.—The principal has charge of the discipline of the school and gives instruction in the theory and practice of teaching.

3.—One of the assistants is the teacher of mathematics, the other of English grammar, geography and history.

4.—The teachers are paid monthly.

5.—The Finance Committee of the Board has charge of all the funds for the support of the Normal School.

ACT No. 65, APPROVED MARCH 21, 1865.

ART. CLXXIV.—FRANKLIN COLLEGE PROPERTY AT OPELOUSAS.

SEC. 1. The Franklin College, at Opelousas, Louisiana, with all its grounds and appurtenances is hereby under the control of the State Board of Education, for the purpose of establishing a normal or high school.

TULANE UNIVERSITY.

Act 43, approved July 5, 1884, to foster, maintain and develop the University of Louisiana.

ART. CLXXV.—BENEFICIARIES.

SEC. 6. That in consideration of the vesting of the administration of the University of Louisiana in the said Administrators of the "Tulane Education Fund;" of the transfer of the rights, powers and privileges, franchises and immunities of the said University to said Administrators, and of the exemption from all taxation as hereinbefore provided, the said Administrators hereby agree and bind themselves.

As an additional consideration between the parties to this Act, the said Board agrees to give continuously, in the academic department, free tuition to one student from each Senatorial and from each Representative district or parish, to be nominated by its members in the General Assembly from among the *bona fide* citizens and residents of his district or parish, who shall comply with the requirements for admission established by said Board. The meaning of this provision being that each member of the General Assembly, whether Senator or Representative shall have the right of appointing one student, in accordance with the foregoing provisions. The free tuition herein provided for shall continue until each student has graduated from the academic department, unless his scholarship has ceased from other causes. Whenever a scholarship becomes vacant, from any cause, the Senator or Representative who appointed the previous student, or his successor, shall in the manner prescribed by this section immediately name a successor.

LOUISIANA STATE UNIVERSITY AND AGRICULTURAL AND MECHANICAL COLLEGE

ACT No. 100, OF THE YEAR 1886.

ART. CLXXVI.—CADETS.—BENEFICIARIES.

SECTION 1. That each parish shall have the right to delegate to the Louisiana State University and Agricultural and Mechanical College, one beneficiary cadet, and that the City of New Orleans shall have the right to delegate to said institution, seventeen beneficiary cadet, or one from each-ward of said city, said beneficiaries to remain at said institution 4 years, unless sooner graduated or otherwise discharged; *provided,* that no beneficiary cadet shall be permitted to resign from said institution without the consent of the board of supervisors thereof, which consent shall be given only in a case of urgent necessity, such as serious and long protracted ill health, duly declared by certificate of the surgeon of said institution or other competent physician, to be of such nature as to render it impossible for said cadet to pursue his studies with advantage.

ART. CLXXVII.—POLICE JURIES AND THE CITY COUNCILS TO ELECT THE BENEFICIARIES.

SEC. 2. That the Police Jury of each parish and the City Council of New Orleans, respectively, may, at a regular meeting, elect the number of beneficiary cadets to which said parish or city is entitled as aforesaid, of such age and qualifications as may be prescribed by the board of supervisors for admission to the college and classes of said University and Agricultural and Mechanical College, and shall cause the beneficiary so elected to report in person at said institution on or before said 5th day of October; *provided.* that said beneficiary cadet shall be selected from the number of these residents of said parish or of said city, who have not themselves, nor have their parents, the means of defraying the whole of their necessary expenses of maintenance and support at said institution, which facts shall be duly certified to the president of said institution by the president of said Police Jury or said City Council of New Orleans as true, to the best of his knowledge and belief.

ART. CLXXVIII.—MAINTENANCE AND BOARD OF BENEFICIARIES.

That for the maintenance and board of said beneficiaries in said institution, the police juries of the several parishes and the City Council of the city of New Orleans be and are hereby authorized and empowered to appropriate out of their respective treasuries a sufficient sum to defray the necessary expenses of said cadets as appointed under the provisions of this act ; *provided*, that the expenses of no cadet shall exceed $250 *per annum*; *provided further*, that under no circumstances shall any part of this sum be paid by the State.

ART. CLXXIX —APPROPRIATION FURTHER AUTHORIZED.

SEC. 5.   That in order to take advantage of the right granted to each parish and to the City. of New Orleans in section 1 of this act, each parish and said city shall make an appropriation of $150 *per annum* out of any money in its treasury for the maintenance and board in said institution of each benefiary cadet delegated by said parish or said city, said sum to be paid to the treasurer of such institution before the admission of said cadet, and the power to make such appropriation is hereby granted to the police juries of the several parishes and to the City Council of New Orleans.

NOTA.—No charges are made for tuition. as this institution whether the cadets. be beneficiaries or not. For further information see act of incorporation.

ACT 49, APPROVED JULY 10, 1888.

ART. CLXXX.—DEAF AND DUMB AND THE BLIND.

SEC. 1.   This institution is united under one management and control.

ART. CLXXXI.—BOARD OF ADMINISTRATORS.

SEC. 2.   Consist of five members, to be appointed every four years by the Governor.

ART. CLXXXII.—SUPERVISION AND CONTROL.

SEC. 3.   Are entrusted to the Board.

ART. CLXXXIII.—INSTRUCTION AND SUPPORT.

SEC. 6.   Are provided for the deaf and dumb and the blind residents of this State, of sound mind and proper health, between the ages of eight and twenty-five, they are entitled to be admitted in this institution as pupils, and to be provided with board, lodging, medicine and medical attendance at the expense of this institution (if they are in indigent circumstances). They may also be furnished with clothing, and with traveling expenses to the institution and from the institution.

ART. CLXXXIV.—TERM FOR WHICH ADMITTED.

SEC. 7.   Pupils admitted between eight and fourteen years of age may continue in the institution eight years—also those admitted between the ages of fourteen and seventeen years, and all admitted at an age exceeding seventeen years may continu five years.   The board may extend the limit two years in each case.

NOTA.—There is a printing department in which the deaf mutes are taught the art of printing.

It is proposed to teach them to work in wood, and give them other manual training; to prepare them to earn self-support and competency by manual labor, at the same time that they are given the advantages of education.

ACT. 87, APPROVED APRIL 10, 1887.

ART. CLXXXV.—SOUTHERN UNIVERSITY.

Under this act the Southern University was established.

The Governor of the State, Samuel D. McEnery, says, in his annual message (1888) in regard to this institution:

"By authority of the General Assembly, granted by Act No. 13, of 1886, the Board of Trustees of the Southern University sold the property on Calliope street, near St. Charles Avenue, in New Orleans, to the McDonongh School Fund for $15,000, and with the proceeds have purchased ample premises on Magazine street, between Dufossat and Soniat streets, and built a large, commodious and beautiful school building, ornamental to the vicinity, and worthy of the noble object of the institution."

This college is intended to give to the colored citizens of Louisiana the means of higher education to their children.

The progress of the students has been satisfactory.

NOTA.—This institution supplies the places of a High School and of a Normal School in the City of New Orleans, respecting the pupils of color.

PEABODY EDUCATIONAL FUND.

ART. CXXXVI.—THE TRUSTEES.

This fund, under the able management of the Trustees, is distributed in accordance with the last will of the Great Philanthropist.

The greater part of the income is used in educating teachers for the public schools.

Aid is given to the State Normal Schools of a high order.

Only free public schools are aided.

The trustees have organized an institution of collegiate grade at Nashville, Tennessee, for the education and professional training of teachers.

The amount allowed each student annually is $200.

Louisiana is favored with eight scholarships.

This year three vacancies have been filled.

The next year there will be five vacancies at this institution.

The applicant must be 17 years of age.

Must produce a satisfactory certificate of moral character, gentlemanly or lady-like habits and presumed good health; must declare his intention of making teaching a profession; must give pledge to remain at the College two years, and to teach in the public schools of his or her own State at least two years if there is an opportunity.

ART. CLXXXVII.—DISTRIBUTION OF THE FUNDS.

The discretion of the Trustees is absolute in distributing the fund. The State Superintendent of Public Education must conform to their rules and regulations.

INDEX

A

ART. II. — Authority and duty of the State Board of Education 17
ART. IX.—Attorney of the Parish Boards.............. 20
ART. XIX.—Accounts the State Superintendent shall keep. 22
ART. XXVII.—Additional compensation allowed for certain services of the Parish Superintendent............... 24
ART. XXXV.—Attendance of the teachers' obligatory.... 26
ART. LXIV.—Authority of the directors Parish of Orleans.. 34

INDEX TO LAWS DATED PRIOR TO ACT 81, AND AUXILIARY THERETO.

ART. LXXVI.—Attorneys may be appointed to protect school interest.................................... 40
ART. LXXX.—Assessors—Annual enumeration of youths. 41
ART. CIV.—Act of the Congress of the U. S. approved February 15th, 1843 47
ART. CXII.—Accumulations and re-investments.......... 55

INDEX TO ACT 81 OF 1872.

ART. CXV.—Abolishment of the school fund 56

INDEX TO DIFFERENT ACTS.

ART. CXXXII.—Auditor to ascertain the amounts due townships.. 66
ART. CLVII.—Amounts paid in error recoverable........ 77
ART. CLXI.—Authority of the Board of Administrators... 78
ART. CLXII.—Appropriations.......................... 78
ART. CLXIII —Annual sessions........................ 78
ART. CLXXIX.—Appropriation further authorized. 84

B

ART. XIV.—Branches to be taught, also the French language in those localities where the French language predominates.................................... 21
ART. XX.—Biennial report and what it shall contain and number of copies to be printed and distributed....... 23
ART. LVII.—Bond of the Treasurer.................... 32
ART. LXXI.—Budget of annual expenses, what it shall include 38
ART. CX...Bonds.................................... 55

ART. CLIII.—Branches of studies............................. 73
ART. CLIX.—Board of administrators.................... 78

INDEX TO ACT 182 OF 1853.

ART. CLXXV.—Beneficiaries...................... 82
ART. CLXXXI.—Board of Administrators 84

C

ART. XXII.—Copies of the State Superintendent's records
and papers admissible in evidence................. 23
ART. XXVIII.—Committee for the selection of teachers.. 24
ART. L.—Certificate required as a requisite to the employ-
ment of a teacher................................... 30
ART. LXII.—City Schools............................... 33

INDEX TO ACT OF JULY 12, 1888, RELATING TO POLL
TAX COLLECTION.

ART. LXXXIV.—Collection of the Poll Tax............. 43

INDEX TO ACT 126 OF 1882.

ART XCV.—Conditions the donor can impose......... 45

INDEX TO DIFFERENT ACTS.

ART. CXXXI.—Capital due the several townships....... 66
ART. CXXXIII.—Current funds for Schools in State treas-
ury 67
ART. CXXXIV.—Capital due the several townspips....... 67
ART. CXXXVI.—Cultivating or inclosing 16th sections.
Penalties.. 68
ART. CXLV.—Certificate to be filed by the teacher........ 71
ART. CXLVII.—Certificates of indebtedness............. 71
ART. CLXV—Course of studies........................ 78
ART. CLXVI.—Condition for admission.................. 78
ART. CLXXVI.—Cadets. Beneficiaries................. 83

D

ART. VII.—Duty and authority of the Parish Boards...... 18
ART. XI.—Divisions of Parishes into school districts..... 20
ART. XV.—Duties of the President of the School Board.... 21
ART. XVIII.—Duties of the State Superintendent and the
schools subject to his supervisory control............ 22
ART. XXIV.—Decisions to be made by the State Superin-
tendent and appeals from his decisions.............. 23

INDEX TO ACT 126 OF 1882.

ART. XCIII—Donations for educational, charitable or literary purposes 45
ART. XCIV.—Donors 45

Art. XCIX.—Duty of the trustees 46
Art. C.—Duty of the trustees respecting other donations.. 46
    INDEX TO U. S. LAWS RELATING TO DONATION.
Art. CIII.—Donation according to Federal representation. 47
    INDEX TO ACT 126 OF 1882.
Art. CXX.—Decision 59
Art. CLXXX.—Deaf and Dumb and the Blind 84
Art. CLXXXVII.—Distribution of the funds............. 86

E

Art. XLIV.—Examination of applicants to be appointed
    teachers, by whom conducted and how 28
Art. XLV.—Examination fee.......................... 29
Art. XLVI.—Examiners, their duties and penalties for non-
    performance...................................... 29
Art. LXIX.—*Ex-Officio* members...................... 37
Art. CXLIV.—Examination of teachers on the subject 71
Art. CLVI.—Error in apportioning school funds.......... 77

F

Art. XLIX.—First grade certificate 29
Art. LV.—Fines and bonds forfeited; to be collected for
    the support of the common school 31
Art. CI.—*Fidei commissae*............................. 47
    INDEX TO U S. LAWS RELATING TO DONATIONS.
Art. CII.—Free schools—Donation..................... 47
Art. CVI.—Funds can be invested by legislative authority. 48
Art. CVIII.—Free school fund 54
    INDEX TO ACT OF C. OF 1879.
Art. CXVI.—Free school fund, seminary fund and agricul-
    tural and mechanical college fund.................. 57
Art. CLXIV.—Faculty 78
Art. CLXXIV.—Franklin College property at Opelousas.. 82

G

Art. X.—Graded and high schools and authority of the
    parochial boards in that connection 20
Art. XCII.—General revenue act...................... 44
    INDEX TO ACT 126 OF 1882.
Art. XCVIII.—Governor may whenever there is a failure
    on the part of the trustees to accept, appoint others.. 46

H

Art. LIX.—How the school fund shall be disbursed....... 32

I

Art. XXI.—Institution of the blind, and the deaf and
    dumb. Reports and suggestions to be made by the
    State Superintendent 23
Art. XXXIX.—Institute managers in the parishes........ 27
Art. XL.—Institute fund. How collected, kept and ex-
    pended 27
Art. XLI.—Institute, not applicable to New Orleans...... 27
Art. XLII.—Institutes ordered to be held by the State
    board. Attendance and how held 27

INDEX TO LAW DATED PRIOR TO ACT 81 OF 1888 AND AUXIL-
                    IARY THERETO.

Art. LXXIX.—Indebtedness of parish school boards, lim-
    ited 41

          INDEX TO ACT 182 OF 1857.

Art. CXI.—Interest 55

          INDEX TO DIFFERENT ACTS.

Art. CXVIII.—Improvement tax 58
Art. CXXXIX.—Illegal certificates of indebtedness 69

          HYGIENE AND TEMPERANCE.

Art. CXLII.—Instruction to be given.................... 70
Art. CLXXXIII.—Instruction and support 84

L

Art. XXXVI.—Length of time for sessions and forfeitures
    for non-attendance................................ 26

INDEX TO ACTS DATED PRIOR TO ACT 81 OF 1888 AND AUXILIARY
                    THERETO.

Art. LXXXIII.—Limit of poll tax...... 43

    INDEX TO LAWS OF THE U. S. RELATIVE TO DONATION.

Art. CV.—Lease of land............................... 48

          INDEX TO ACT 126 OF 1882.

Art. CXXVIII.—Lease of land 63
Art. CLI.—Legal authorities on the subject of school dis-
    cipline.................................. 72

M

Art. XXXVII.—Members of these Institutes may be honorary or active 26
Art. CXXX.—Mode of annulling sales 64
Art. CLXXVIII.—Maintenance and Board of Beneficiaries. 83

N

Art. XXIII.—Neglect of duty to be reported and the improper use of the school funds 23

INDEX TO LAWS DATED PRIOR TO ACT 81 OF 1888 AND AUXILIARY THERETO.

Art. LXXVIII.—Negotiable evidence of debts cannot be issued 40
Art. CL.—Notice to be issued by the Auditor............. 72
Art. CLVIII.—Normal Schools at Natchitoches........... 77
Art. CLXXII.—New Orleans Normal School.............. 80

O

Art. XIII.—Option when school districts adjoin as to which school certain children will attend 21
Art. XXXII.—Oaths they may administer............... 26
Art. XXXIII.—Office days of the Parish Superintendent.. 26
Art. LXIII.—Organization of the Board and salary....... 33

P

Art. III.—Parochial boards of school directors, rules for the government of schools and the uniformity of text books 17
Art. IV.—Parish Superintendent; additional report may be required of him by the State Board of Education.. 18
Art. XXV.—Parish Superintendent................... 24
Art. LIV.—Police Juries and all municipal corporations except New Orleans to levy 1½ mills for school purposes in their annual budget...................... 31
Art. LXXII.—Provisions for affording proper evidence of claim 39

INDEX TO ACTS PRIOR TO ACT 81 OF 1888 AND AUXILIARY THERETO.

Art. LXXXI.—Parish Superintendent's duty respecting enumeration of youths........................... 41

Art. LXXXII.—Poll tax 42

INDEX TO ACT 89 OF 1888 RELATING TO POLL TAX.

Art. LXXXVI.—Penalties 43

INDEX TO ACT 126 OF 1882.

Art. XCVI —Property cannot be made inalienable.....:... 46

INDEX TO ACT 182 OF 1857.

Art. CIX.—Perpetual and trust fund to bear six per cent interest *per annum*............................. 55
Art. CXXI.—Publication 59
Art. CXXIX.—Proceeds of lands accruing to townships... 64
Art. CXLVI.—Postponement in some respect of the enforcement of part of the law........................ 71
Art. CXLIX —Provision further upon the subject 72
Art. CLXX.—Proceeds of the sale — how to be appropriated 80
Art. CLXXIII. — Plan of organization of the Normal School..................................... 81
Art. CLXXVII.— Police Juries and the City Councils to elect the beneficiaries.......................... 83

R

Art. VIII.— Removal of Parish Superintendents and their appeals ....:..................................... 19
Art. XXIX.—Report of school children in each parish and district, when to be made and by whom 25
Art. XXX.—Report annually by the Parish Superintendent, to whom made, when, what it shall contain and penalty for failure to make the report.. 25
Art. XXXI.—Record they shall keep, description of school districts, custody of papers and documents.......... 25
Art. XXXVIII.—Roll of members.......... 27
Art. XLIII.— Reports to be made by Parish Superintendents respecting institutes........................ 28
Art. LI.— Register and report to be made monthly by teachers 30
Art. LIII.—Revenue .. .:................................ 30
Art. LXI.—Receipts and disbursements, account of, when required and how be made 33
Art. LXX.—Report of the Board, when and to whom made, its contents 37
Art. LXXIII.—Restrictions on contracts and debts.. 39
Art. LXXIV.—Repeal of all conflicting clauses........... 39

INDEX TO LAWS ADOPTED PRIOR TO ACT 81 OF 1888
AND AUXILIARY THERETO.

Art. LXXVII.—Rights of free passage over streams, etc.. 40

INDEX TO ACT OF 89 1888, RELATING TO THE POLL TAX.

ART. LXXXV.—Return of collections to be made by the sheriffs and tax collectors 43
ART. LXXXVII.—Rule to show cause of non-compliance.. 44

INDEX TO ACT, JULY 1886, NO. 87.

ART. LXXXVIII.—Receipt required 44
ART. XC.—Report to be made by the Clerk of Court or other officer 44
ART. XCI.—Revenues from local taxation................ 44

INDEX TO ACT 182 OF 1857.

ART. CXIII.—Rent of 16th section to be paid to Parish Treasurers 56
ART. CLV.—Rate of compensation to teachers 76
ART. CLX.—Residence of the Members of the Board 78
ART. CLXXI.—Repealing clause......................... 80

S

ART. I.— State Board of Public Education................ 17
ART. VI.— School Boards are bodies corporate..... 18
ART. XII.— School districts in two adjoining parishes, how laid off.. 21
ART. XVI.— State Superintendent of Public Education 22
ART. XVII.—Salary of the State Superintendent, his office, stationery, clerk and porter 22
ART. XLVIII.—Second grade certificate.................. 29
ART. LII.—Studies prescribed by the board to be followed and accountability of pupils to teachers............. 30
ART. LVI.—School treasurer............................ 31
ART. LXV.— Services of city board shall be rendered without compensation.......................... 36
ART. LXVI.— Superintendent of New Orleans city schools, his duties, authority, salary 36

INDEX TO LAWS DATED PRIOR TO ACT 81 OF 1888, STITL IN FORCE AND AUXILIARY TO THAT ACT.

ART. LXXV.— State and Parish Boards cannot be compelled to give bond and security in suits............. 39

INDEX TO DECISION OF THE STATE COURTS.

ART. CVII.— State a trustee 48

INDEX TO ACT 126 OF 1882.

ART. CXIX.— Special tax, how levied................... 58
ART. CXXII.— School house and public improvement 59
ART. CXXIII.— School lands. Their sales. How to be made. Duty of Parish Treasurer respecting public school lands 62
ART. CXXIV.—Survey of school lands 62

ART. CXXV.—Sale on the order of the Auditor...........   62
ART. CXXVI.—Sale of sections, divided by lines of par-
    ishes.....   63
ART. CXXXVII.—School property exempt from seizure...   68
ART. CXXXVIII.—Sixteenth sections and court decisions
    respecting them...................................   68
ART. CXLI.— Sales of sixteenth sections   69
ART. CLIV.—School Directors...........................   73
ART. CLXVII.—Site of Normal School in New Orleans un-
    der control of State Board of Education.............   79
ART. CLXVIII.—State Board of Education—Right to sell.   79
ART. CLXXXII.—Supervision and control...............   84
ART. CLXXXV.—Southern University   85

T

ART. V.—Term of office of the members of the Parish
    Boards and of the Parish Superintendents   18
ART. XXXIV.— Teachers' institute or association   26
ART. XLVII.— Third grade certificate...................   29
ART. LVIII.— Transfer of school funds..................   32
ART. LX.— Treasurer's compensation   33
ART. LXVII — Treasurer of New Orleans, ex-Officio treasu-
    rer of the Board, his bond........................   36
ART. LXVIII.— Treasurer's office, removal, successor, sal-
    ary...   37
    INDEX TO ACT 87 OF 1886, RELATING TO POLL TAX.
ART. LXXXIX. —Tax (poll) to be deducted if receipt be not
    produced   44
        INDEX TO ACT 126 OF 1882.
ART. XCVII.—Trustees to organize in a body corporate...   46
        INDEX TO ACT OF 182 OF 1857.
ART. CXIV.—Trust Fund   56
    INDEX TO ACT OF THE CONSTITUTION AUTHORIZING
        THE INCREASE OF TAXATION.
ART. CXVII.— Taxation possible to erect and construct
    public buildings.................   58
ART. CXXVII.—Treasurer's commission   63
ART. CXXXV.—Timber on sixteenth section. Cutting or
    burning same   68
ART. CXLIII.—Text books..............................   70
ART. CLII.—Teachers' judgment about discipline   73
ART. CLXIX.—To authorize the State Board of Education
    to sell certain property...........................   80
ART. CLXXXIV.—Term for which admitted   85
ART. CLXXXVI.—The Trustees..........................   85

V

Art. XXVI.—Visits to be made 24

W

Art. CXLVIII.—Warrants issued under the preceding section 71

RULES AND REGULATIONS

ADOPTED BY

The State Board of Education,

STATE OF LOUISIANA,

FOR THE

GOVERNMENT OF THE PUBLIC SCHOOLS.

———

RULE I. The elementary schools in cities and towns shall contain at least six grades, viz:—first, second, third (and possibly fourth), primary and first and second Grammar Departments; but such changes may be made by the local board as the condition of the locality may require.

RULE II.—In the primary departments there shall be taught: spelling, reading, phonetics, writing, geography, arithmetic and object lessons.

In the Grammar Departments, thorough instruction shall be given if the derivation of words, dictation, reading, writing, arithmetic, grammar, geography, history, elocution, composition, declamation, the natural sciences, and when possible, vocal and instrumental music, also drawing. It is recommended that the French language be taught in those localities, where the French population predominates, *provided*, the expenses of the school are not increased.

RULE III.—The High School, or Central School shall continue the instruction of such youths as can pursue such studies as will best prepare them for admission to the Normal Schools, or to the freshmen class of Tulane University and the freshman class of the Louisiana State University and A. & M. College.

RULE IV.—The Normal Schools shall have for object the professional training of young men and women as teachers for the common schools of the State, and to thereby improve the standard of the public schools.

SCHOOL SESSIONS.

RULE V.—The scholastic year shall commence on the first Monday in January, and the schools shall continue open during the session and during such times as the local board may deem proper.

RULE VI.—The daily sessions shall not be less than five hours.

EXAMINATION OF TEACHERS.

RULE VII.—A public examination shall be held at least once each year. All the classes in the High Schools and Normal Schools shall be examined in writing in each branch of study when it is completed.

VACATIONS AND HOLIDAYS.

RULE VIII.—The schools shall be closed on Saturdays and Sundays, and on such other days as may be directed by the Parish Boards.

TEACHERS.

RULE IX.—Teachers shall be at their respective rooms at least 15 minutes before the hour of opening each session, and shall, in their daily registers, to be kept by the Principal, record the names and the time of arrival of each teacher; and any teacher not complying, shall be reported to the local superintendent, for such action as he may see proper under the laws, rules and regulations.

During any recess or intermission, the teachers shall remain on the school grounds, or in the premises.

RULE X.—The jurisdiction and authority of the teacher over the pupils shall not be limited to the school house or enclosures nor to the actual session of the school. Generally in matters connected with the schools and the manners and morals of the scholars, his authority, with that of the parent, commences when pupils leave the parental roof and control, to go to school, and shall continue until their return from school. The teacher however, shall not be responsible for the misconduct of pupils on the way to and from school, though he shall have the right to punish for misconduct when brought to his knowledge.

RULE XI.—The teachers shall bestow equal and impartial attention on all their pupils. They shall maintain discipline and pay regard to the morals of their pupils.

RULE XII.—It shall be their duty to practice such discipline in their schools as would be exercised by a kind and judicious parent in his family, always firm and vigilant but prudent. They shall endeavor on all proper occasions, to impress upon the minds of their pupils the principle of morality and virtue; a sacred regard for truth, reverence for the Creator, respect for one another, rectitude, industry and frugality. But no teacher shall exercise any sectarian or political influence in the school.

They shall see that all pupils under their charge distinctly understand all rules relating to pupils, and they shall teach them the rules of health—hygiene and the bad effects of narcotics, as required by Act No. 40 of the General Assembly of 1888.

RULE XIII.—Any teacher who may be absent from school on account of sickness or other necessity must cause immediate notice to be given to the local superintendent. Teachers absent three consecutive days without cause may be considered as having abandoned their positions.

RULE XIV.—No teacher shall resign without giving two weeks notice to the local superintendent, else he may be made to forfeit one half month's pay.

RULE XV.—Teachers shall not hold any position of higher grade than the one corresponding to their certificates, nor shall the salary be larger than that allowed to the grade in which they teach.

RULE XVI.—All teachers shall attend the State and Parish Institutes, when notified by their superintendent.

PRINCIPAL TEACHERS.

RULE XVII.—The principal teachers shall keep a register, in which they shall record the name, age, birth place, residence, the names of the parents or guardians of each pupil entering the public schools, also the occupation of the parent or guardian.

RULE XVIII.—The principals shall be required within one week after the commencement of each term, to have the programme of their daily exercises posted in the school room, in a conspicuous place, and shall transmit a copy to the local superintendent and one to the State superintendent.

RULE XIX.—They shall keep a daily record of all pupils admitted; those present, those absent or tardy. They shall, at the end of each month, report the condition of their respective schools to the local superintendent, and file, in his office, a copy of their respective registers, and, at the close of the school year, shall forward a certified copy of said register to the State Board of Education; they shall also keep records and make reports as required by Act No. 81, of the year 1888.

RULE XX.—The principal shall have supervisory control of the grounds, buildings and appliances, also, furniture and other common school property, and shall be held responsible for any want of neatness or cleanliness of the premises.

Whenever repairs are needed, the president of the school board should be notified by him.

PUPILS' ADMISSION.

RULE XXI.—Children entering the public schools are required to furnish all the necessary text-books and stationary used in their classes. The pupils are to be admitted in the primary schools not younger than six years. A pupil can begin school only on the first day of each week, and is to be be accompanied at the time of his admission, by one of his parents, or guardian, or by a friend who will see to the proper registry of his name and furnish any further needtul information.

RULE XXII.—They must attend the school established in the local school district in which they reside, or such school as the local board may designate.

RULE XXIII.—All transfers within the schools, or from one school to another, rendered necessary for any cause, shall be made by authority of the local superintendent. Pupils wishing transfers, must produce certificates from their former teachers, stating their reasons and the class to which they belonged.

RULE XXIV.—No pupil shall be admitted to school after ten o'clock, or be allowed to depart before the appointed hour, except in case of sickness, or for other cause in the judgment of the teacher.

RULE XXV.— No pupil shall be admitted to the High School, unless he has undergone a sufficient and satisfactory examination.

DIRECTIONS TO SCHOOL OFFICERS AND OTHERS CON-

NECTED WITH THE PUBLIC SCHOOLS.

RULE XXVI.— Officers connected with the department of public schools, and all the employees are earnestly requested, indeed directed, to exert every resonable endeavor to the promotion of the schools. They should avoid all antagonism and unkind opposition, but should never fail whenever opportunity offers, to exercise their influence in behalf of a system that gives to many youths of our State, the opportunity of escaping from the benighted condition of the absolutely illiterate.

In all matters of revenue for the schools, they should always endeavor to create a healthy condition, thereby assisting in setting aside (without its being a burden to any one) a sufficient amount to maintain the school system as it should be.

By co-operative action the schools will become the pride of the State and reflect its excellence, and the contributors will be more than rewarded by the improved condition.

RULES FOR THE EXAMINATION OF TEACHERS.

I.--Teachers shall not be examined to teach nor be given a certificate unless they enjoy a good moral character.

The committee of examiners shall cause teachers to appear before them and be examined in the branches they are to teach.

II.--The examination, when two or more apply, for the same position, shall be competitive; the questions shall be answered in writing in presence of the examiners, in all branches in which such an examination is practicable.

III.--The written answers shall be examined. the merit marks or figures noted, and the candidate receiving the largest aggregate shall be preferred, *provided*, he is found competent.

IV.--A record of examination shall be kept by the local superintendent and shall be subject to the inspection of any officer connected with the schools.

V.--Candidates shall be classified as follows, viz :

1st.--The central or High School Grade.

2nd.--Principals in the grammar departments.

3rd.--Assistants in the grammar departments.

4th.--Those in the primary departments, with such salaries in each department or grades as the School Board deem proper.

5th.--Public notice should always be given of the day the examination will be held.

6th.--The appointee may be given charge of a school on probation during a period not longer than one month, during which time, permanent engagement may be made,--else he should not be employed, but paid for the services rendered.

OUTLINE OF STUDIES.

____

UNGRADED SCHOOLS.

" The Superintendent of Education shall, whenever required, give advice, explanation, construction or information to officers and others, relative to the management of the schools and all other questions calculated to promote the cause of education." Section 24, Act 81, of the year 1888.

In presenting the following outline of studies it is not intended to be mandatory upon teachers, but they are urgently advised to follow this outline, unless they are certain that their own curriculum is preferable.

A course of studies is prepared with very little judgment, that is not a decided improvement on none at all.

It should be understood that this outline is not presented as anything especially original.

It is the result of selections made after considerable attention had been given to the subject.

In organizing a school, the pupils should be classed as near as possible in accordance with the course of studies adopted.

A programme of daily exercises should be prepared.

The work should be reviewed *frequently*, and examinations should be made.

Rules for examination should be adopted, and promotions made at stated times after a course of studies have been thoroughly followed.

In classifying, it is convenient to make the grade conform to the readers.

The first grade should correspond to the time the child reads the first reader.

The second grade, the second reader. And so on to and including the fifth reader.

One year will be sufficient time to follow the first grade course, and a similar time for the second grade.

The third and fourth require more time, generally.

Fixed rules cannot very well be prescribed

In every instance a systematic plan of work should be adopted, whether it conforms to the outline or not makes little difference, but we must impress upon teachers the importance of classification and of following a well defined outline of studies.

A settled guide is desirable always, but this does not imply that the teacher should *servilely* follow a model. Diversity and departure from the beaten track are at times quite useful and improving.

Tuition that is nothing but routine, and, as it were, mechanical work, will bring about very little if any beneficial results.

Much must be left to the judgment, the invention and intellectual sympathy of the teacher.

He will by close observation and experience. learn the nature and educable ability of his children and the instruction they need, and then calmly reason out and determine upon the plan best adapted to impart this instruction.

In this, to be successful, he will have to adopt well defined methods.

The object of this appendix is not so much to direct attention to a course of studies to be adopted and an outline of work to be followed, but to particularly remind the teacher that some method must be followed or his labors will fall far short of the usefulness they should have.

FIRST CLASS.

TIME ALLOWED, NINE MONTHS.

Familiar words as wholes, in print, presenting the object or its picture if necessary to give the pupils a clear conception of the meaning; pupils construct sentences containing only these words.
Pupils copy on blackboard and slates.
Written words taught after thorough drill in printed words.
Simple sounds of letters—First reader, about twenty pages.
Long and short vowel sounds and sounds of consonants.
Phonic analysis of words. Words of regular formation.
Alphabet—Complete First reader.
Review first reader. If possible read another first reader.
Let supplementary reading be furnished the child.
The first steps are important and should be correctly taken.
They should be taught to observe objects.
Easy and suggestive questions should be propounded.

In teaching, use the words and phonic methods in combination, lead the children to recognize the sounds of which words are composed, and write sounds into spoken words; do not force this upon the children, but make them self active.

Write upon the blackboard names of familiar objects, and teach the child to recognize the words and pronounce correctly as soon as pointed out. Keep a list of words learned upon the blackboard, and add new words as soon as learned. Review these words daily.

The pronunciation of words is not reading, but the preparatory exercise. The children should be able to understand clearly the meaning of the words.

The teaching of new written words, and then combining them into sentences, should be continued until the child has learned to "take in" a short sentence at a glance, and read it with ease.

SECOND CLASS.

LANGUAGE.

READING AND PHONICS.

Conversations on subjects attractive to young pupils.
Train them to speak in complete sentences.
Make grammatical sentences about familiar objects.
Spell by writing all words in the reading lessons.

ARITHMETIC.

Teach counting and adding objects, as balls on the numeral frame, &c., &c.

All possible combinations of numbers to 7.

Some of the combinations of 4, are given below.

1 and 1 and 1 and 1.

2 and 2.	4 divided by 2.
3 and 1.	4 divided by 4.
1 and 3.	4 divided by 1.
1 and 2 and 1.	4 divided by 3.
1 and 1 and 2.	$\frac{1}{4}$ of 4.
2 and 1 and 1.	$\frac{2}{4}$ of 4.
4 times 1.	$\frac{3}{4}$ of 4.
2 times 2.	$\frac{1}{2}$ of 4.
1 time 3 and 1.	$\frac{2}{2}$ of 4.
1 time 4.	4 quarts make 1 gallon.
	4 pecks make 1 bushel.

Similar combinations should be made with other numbers.

When number is referred to as applied to the work of children first entering schools, distinguish between applied or concrete number and abstract or pure number.

All true teaching begins on the foundation already laid in the mind of the child, and advances the work by intelligent measures as the mind develops.

The teacher should see that the school room is supplied with objects for teaching numbers, and these are readily obtained.

Beans, sticks, pieces of pasteboard, squares and triangles of pasteboard cost nothing; flowers and leaves, any common object, with little ingenuity, represent to the mind of the child, cattle, horses, birds, peanuts, &c, and thus the work of teaching the combinations will become a pleasure to both instructor and instructed.

Don't begin the written book or the combination of abstract numbers till some skill has been gained by hands and eyes in separating and discerning.

The early use of abstract numbers will lead the child into the error of confounding figures with numbers which they represent. The teacher should make a clear distinction between numbers and their signs, and should never treat figures and numbers as identical.

Before passing on from number 4, see that the child recognizes readily the number of objects when held before him; that he can select four objects from a number of objects before him; that he can select the ½, ¼ and ¾ of 4; that he can make the groups of objects which together make 4, or can be taken from 4.

Have all patience with the tedious work in the beginning. The success of much after work depends upon the thoroughness acquired here.

A possible combinations of numbers to 10, objectively and abstractly.

Counting to 100, and by 2's and 5's to 50.

The fractional parts of all numbers to 10.

Have pupils make table of combinations to 10 — similar to the following:

```
1 & 1 & 1 & 1 & 1 & 1 & 11 multiplied by 8.
2 " 2 " 2 " 2          1      "        " 6 and 2
3 " 3 " 2              8 minus 2
2 " 3 " 3              8   "    4
3 " 2 " 3              8   "    8
4 and 4               8   "    1
5   "  3              8   "    3
3   "  5              8   "    5
5   "  2 and 1        8   "    7
1   "  2 "  5       8 divided by 7
2   "  1 "  5       8   "    "   5
6   "  2            8   "    "   2
2   "  6            8   "    "   1
6   "  1 and 1      8   "    "   3
7   "  1            8   "    "   6 .
1   "  7            8   "    "   8
8 multiplied by 1   8   "    "   4
4   "        "  2   ½, ²⁄₂, ¼, ²⁄₄, ¾, ⁴⁄₄, ⅛ ⎫
2   "        "  4                          ⎬ of 8.
3   "        "  2 and 2                    ⎭
1   "        "  7 " 1.
```

The number 7, suggest number of days in a week, and other facts which should be taught. 8-teach number of quarts in a peck.

The teaching of decimals might commence at this time.

Teach combination of numbers to 12, counting by 3's, 4's and 5's to 100.

Teach fractional parts.

Teach forms as:

```
    2
    3          2 | 10         10     5
    7          ------          6     3
   ----           5          ----  ----
    12                          4    15
```

4 pints make quarts.
6 pecks make bushels.
2 gallons make quarts.
9 feet make yards.

COUNTING AND ADDING—OBJECT LESSONS.

Form.—Common shapes, as square, oblong, ball, cylinder and cube; different kinds of corners and lines.

Color.— Common colors, as red, yellow, blue, green, orange and purple to be distinguished.

Objects.—Names of common objects, their uses and principal parts.

DRAWING AND WRITING.

On Slates.— Simple combinations of straight lines. Writing simple letters.

SECOND READER.

Drill in pronunciation and in learning the meaning of words should be continued.

Give attention to the meaning of sentences and to the general ideas contained in the lesson.

Give dictation exercises.

Every reading lesson should be a lesson in language.

First upon distinct articulation and natural tones.

Teach them to read as they would talk.

In assigning a reading lesson, have all new words pronounced by the class and spelled orally before any attempt to study it, so the pupils will not hesitate or stumble over words while reciting.

Teach the diacritical marks for vowel and consonant sounds, drill carefully in these.

Before beginning the Third Reader, test the pupil's ability to read in some other Second Reader than his own. This rule holds good for all the grades.

Supplementary reading of the proper character should be furnished in this grade also.

1. Write and spell orally.
2. Spell monosyllables by sound.
3. Dictate sentences containing prominent words in lesson.
4. Require exactness in the use of capital letters and punctuation in all written work.

ARITHMETIC.

FUNDAMENTAL RULES AND ROMAN NOTATION.

Combination of numbers through to 15, writing and reading numbers.

Roman notation.

Mental questions, simple and practical, which require the adding of numbers from 5 to 9, to numbers below 30, also subtracting similar numbers.

Combinations through to 18.
Read and write numbers to 100,000.
Review.
All combinations to 20.
Add and subtract numbers containing from two to five places.
Divide, using divisors from 1 to 12.
Multiply numbers from two to five places, using multiplier; from 1 to 12.

The power to readily perceive the sum of two digital numbers and the difference between either of two digital numbers and their sum, is the basis of accurate and rapid computation.

DRAWING AND WRITING.

On Slates.— Copying of reading lessons, plain figures continued. (Designs furnished by teacher.)
On Paper.—Copy-book, No. 1 and 2.

THIRD CLASS.

TIME ALLOWED, NINE MONTHS.

LANGUAGE.

Continue to familiarize pupils with unfamiliar or difficult words, and have them to write sentences containing these words, i. e.

Train them to express the thoughts of the author in language entirely their own. Question carefully in the lesson to awaken thought on the part of the pupils—when? how? what for? &c.

Drill on phonic sounds.

Read selections requiring attention in articulation.

Teach pupils to define reading, accent, emphasis, pitch, punctuation marks, root-word, derivative word, and the use of pauses, viz: comma, period, interrogation point, apostrophe, hyphen, quotation.

Impress the use of the above by writing selections on the board and requiring the pupils to copy, capitalizing and punctuating.

The class should encourage selections, gems of thought.

Phonics.—Words analyzed by sounds. Faults in enunciation corrected.

Continue sentence building.

Teach use of "this" and "that," "is" and "are," "was" and "were," "has" and "have," also singular and plural forms of common name-words and action-words, giving sentences illustrating change in the action-words when the subject changes its number.

Simple rules for punctuation and capitalization.

1. Spell with or without spelling-book.
2. Spell principal words in the reading lessons.
3. Define many words giving easy definitions.

4. Require the phonic spelling for occasional words.
5. Most of the spelling should be written.
6. Continue dictation.
7. Require correct punctuation.

ARITHMETIC.

DRAWING AND WRITING.

On Paper. — Designs (straight lines) furnished by teacher. Copy-book No. 3

1. Review notation and numeration.
2. Read and write numbers to billions.
3. Count by 4's, 5's, 6's, 7's, 8's and 9's to 100.
4. Factoring. *a.* prime factors; *b.* divisors; *c.* greatest common divisor; *d.* least common multiple.

Drill should be given in all the operations of factoring.

5. Common fractions. *a.* definitions; *b.* relative values, using drill tables, as follows:

Units	Halves	Fourths	Eighths	Sixteenths
	$\frac{1}{2}$	$\frac{2}{4}$	$\frac{4}{8}$	$\frac{x}{16}$
1	$\frac{2}{2}$	$\frac{3}{4}$	$\frac{5}{8}$	$\frac{16}{16}$
$1\frac{1}{2}$	$\frac{3}{2}$	$\frac{6}{4}$	$\frac{12}{8}$	$\frac{24}{16}$
2	$\frac{4}{2}$	$\frac{7}{4}$	$\frac{16}{8}$	$\frac{32}{16}$

Require the pupils to make similar tables, showing the relative values of fractions, using $\frac{1}{3}$, $\frac{1}{5}$, $\frac{1}{7}$, &c.

c. Reduction of fractions; *d.* addition; *e.* subtraction; *f.* multiplication; *g.* division.

The pupils should familiarize themselves with the principle in every instance.

6. Decimal fractions. *a.* difference between common and decimal fractions; *b.* notation and numeration; *c.* distinction between tens and tenths, hundreds and hundredths, &c., with their relative positions, with reference to the decimal point; *d.* results of annexing and prefixing ciphers to decimals; *e.* rules for pointing off in multiplication and division of decimals.

7. Denominate numbers *a.* definitions

U. S. or decimal currency. *e.* table.

Tables of weights, measures, etc., completed and reviewed with practical illustrations and simple applications.

GEOGRAPHY.

Teach cardinal and semi-cardinal points of the compass.

Teach geography of the school room, giving relative directions of one object from another.

Exercise in facing and pointing in the various directions.

By actual measurement, teach measurements to estimate distances, as the foot, yard and rod.

Make sketches of school-yard and its neighborhood.

Get as accurately as possible the relative directions and distances.

Geography of the section of country, teaching name, size, location of villages, churches, school-houses and other objects of local interest.

Sketch: Draw a map of the school-room, school-yard, &c., on a difinite scale, as one inch to the foot, or an inch to the yard.

Teach matters of local interest.

The teaching should be as oral as possible, to this time.

Teach surface, level or sloping, plane surface, hill, mountain, ridges of hills, mountain ranges, &c.

FOURTH CLASS.

TIME ALLOWED, NINE MONTHS.

LANGUAGE.

In every reading lesson seek to develop thought and an intelligent comprehension of the selection.

Teach the pupils to give substance of lesson in their own language, and require occasional compositions on topics assigned from the lesson.

Teachers should carefully outline the subject of composition until pupils attain some proficiency in the work.

Have the different words of each lesson spelled, and defined at least one day before assigning the lesson as a reading lesson. These words should be selected by the teacher and written on the blackboard for pupils to copy.

Exercises in word analysis and synonyms should receive daily atrention.

1. Extend the definition work.
2. Spell words by sound.
3. Give occasional lessons requiring the proper sound of the vowels used.
4. Analyze words.
5. Weekly oral reviews are recommended.

Pupils should commence their systematic language work with the third grade.

Construct and analyze simple sentences.

Distinguish between the object and the name-word.

Teach the different parts of speech; classes of nouns, adjectives and adverbs; possessive modifier and noun in apposition.

ARITHMETIC.

1. Linear measure.		2. Square measure.	
3. Cubic "		4. Liquid "	
5. Dry "		6. Troy "	
7. Avoirdupois weight.		8. Time "	
9. Board and lumber measure.			

Mental drill.—Practical problems involving several steps of reasoning, including daily drill in rapid combinations.

Written.—Problems in and outside of text-book to correspond with mental drill.

Percentage—*A*, definition; *b*, sign; *c*, base; *d*, rate; *e*, percentage; *f*, amount; *g*, difference.

Teach thoroughly the principles involved in the five cases in percentage.

Applications of percentage, as those in which time is not an element, 1 trade discount; 2 profit and loss; 3 commissions; 4 insurance; 5 taxes; 6 duties.

GEOGRAPHY.

Teach the geography of the State.
The following is suggested :
1. Size. *a*. length; *b*. breadth; *c*. area; *d*. number of parishes.
2. Boundaries. Separating waters.
3. Climate.
4. Productions. Agricultural; trees, soil, grains, vegetables, fruits, foods; minerals, domestic animals, wild animals, birds, races of men, occupations.
5. Rivers.
6. Lakes.
7. Scenery. Explain what is meant by, *a*. principal meridians; *b*. townships. How townships are designated by number and range. 2. Size. 3. How divided, unite sections. Sections how numbered.
8. Make careful sketch of the State, both on the blackboard and on paper, showing the principal cities, rivers and railroads. Make sketches large, neat and accurate.

A good map of the State should be used in this work.

Care should be given to develop the idea of relative distance and size. Compare the wards with parishes, townships with parishes, and the parishes with the State, and the State with surrounding States.

HISTORY.

United States.—Early discoveries and settlements taught without text book.

WRITING AND DRAWING.

Analysis of letters. Practice paper and copy-book No. 3 and 4. *Blank-books.*—Designs (curve lines) furnished by teacher.

FIFTH CLASS.

TIME ALLOWED, NINE MONTHS.

LANGUAGE.

Suggestions heretofore made apply to this grade.
Give exercises in changing poetry to prose.

Excourage pupils to read selections from standard authors, and to learn something of the authors.

Correct a desire for light and worthless literature.

Careful attention should be given in reading to the cultivation of pure and natural tones of voice.

1. Complete the spelling book.
2. Combine work of other grades in reviews.
3. Demand attention to neatness, legibility and rapidity.
4. Proper names in history and geography should receive attention.

Review work of third grade.

Introduce particles and infiniteness.

The next step will be to make the pupils familiar with the different modes of expanding a sentence by the use of modifiers.

Teach the different kinds of sentences; the properties of nouns and pronouns, including person, number, gender and case; transitive and intransitive verbs, voice and tense.

1. Applications of percentage in which time is a factor.
2. Interest, definition.
3. Discount. *b.* present worth; *c.* bank discount; *d.* difference between true and bank discount.
4. Partial payments. Teach United States rule.
5. Stocks and investments. Definition, *a.* stocks; *b.* par value; *c.* premium; *d.* discount; *e.* brokerage; *f.* dividend.
6. Exchange. *a.* foreign; *b.* domestic.
7. Ratio.
8. Proportion. Simple. Compound.
9. Partnership.
10. Involution and evolution.
11. Government Lands. *a.* how surveyed; *b.* meaning of range; *c.* township; *d.* section; describe the parts of the section.
12 Longitude and time.
13. Mensuration.
14. Metric system.
15. Business Forms, negotiable notes, non negotiable notes, joint note, *in solido*, receipts. 1, per payment of account; in settlement; order for money; checks, 1. Payable to bearer. 2. Payable to order. 3. Certified checks; *a.* certificate of deposit; *b.* due bill; *c.* draft.

It should be the aim of the teacher to cultivate in the child the ability to reason, and to develop the power to make computations quickly and accurately.

Practical problems should be given whenever a new topic is presented, and the child should be drilled upon the topic until he has mastered it, and can apply the operations to practical business problems.

The work should be thoroughly done.

Require the pupil to give a lucid explanation of every problem solved, every step. the idea expressed in every sentence should be understood, and every problem should be intelligently solved.

Study the earth, size and shape.

Note the continents and oceans, and the islands.

Fix their relations to each other. Bound them.

Study the shapes and relative sizes of the different continents. Use a globe, if possible. Care should be taken that the pupil shall conceive of the globe as a representation of the earth and not as the ultimate object of study.

The teacher should assign each lesson carefully, in regular order, indicating all that the pupil is expected to learn.

Sketch carefully the continents, showing the principal rivers and mountain ranges.

To assist in sketching accurately, learn the latitude and longitude of ten places on the coast and three or four in the interior.

Take as a sample lesson South America, begin with Aspinwall on the isthmus and note Gulf of Darien, Corthagena, Magdalena river, Bogota, Cape Gallinas, Lake Maracaybo, Valencia, Trinidad Island, Orinoco River, &c. Let facts of interest connected with these places be given.

The pupils by sketches should show on the blackboard the shape of coast and rivers, and the relative location of places.

By light dotted lines indicate the following parallels: 10 North; Equator 10, 20, 30, 40, 50 South, making the lines parallel. In like manner indicate meridian 40, 50, 60, 70, 80, West, giving the lines the proper curve.

Notice that the space between meridians on parallel sixty is just one half that on the Equator. Locate the points of latitude and longitude learned, and draw the intervening outlines.

Next trace and sketch North America in similar manner.

Trace the British Isles and the western and southern coasts of Europe, and briefly the remaining continents.

MATHEMATICAL GEOGRAPHY.

Define carefully, point, line, surface, plane, sphere, circle, circumference, diameter, meridian, parallel, axis, poles, equator, tropics and polar circles. Define the first eight.

These and the following, tropics will need to be thoroughly reviewed, and many exercises will need to be introduced to see that all of the class have formed true conceptions. It is not enough to recite the exact words.

Circles are planes, not lines. Circles go through the earth, not around it. Equator and tropical circles are realities. Latitude is measured on the circumference of meridians, which are all of the same size. Longitude is measured on the circumference of the equator and parallels : the circumference of parallel sixty contains just one half as many miles as that of the equator.

Use globe.

Give carefully five or six reasons for considering the earth a sphere. Show by calculations that the mountains make the surface less rough.

Give four reasons for believing the earth a spheroid instead of a perfect sphere.

k

Show the position of the earth's axis in respect to the plane of the orbit. Let it be seen what would be the effect on day and night, and the reasons, if the axis were perpendicular to the plane. Show how the axis is declined from the perpendicular. Show how its inclination determines the tropics, polar circles and zones.

Explain the peculiarities of day and night; why the days and nights are always equal at the equator; why they are everywhere equal at the time of the equinoxes.

Explain the phenomena of the seasons. Show why the heat of summer and the cold of winter are the greatest after the tropic is passed.

In explaining some of these phenomena, drawings or apparatus may be used with profit; but no one ever thoroughly understands the subject till he can see the relations of things by a pure act of the mind, power of conception.

This subject is left till the fifth grade, because it is not a subject which the minds of the children are prepared to understand.

HISTORY.

I.   Purposes of the study.

1.   To create in pupils a taste for historical reading and study.

2.   To inform pupils as to books to be read, and to methods of reading and study.

3.   The acquisition of knowledge; a. which shall serve as a basis for future reading and study; b. which shall enable the pupil to understand historical references in general reading.

II.   General plan of teaching.

1.   Select some topic for study.

2   Reproduction by the pupils, both orally and in writing, of the substance of what has been read.

3.   Always use maps to fix locations.

III.   Columbus — sketch of life, theories, voyages. Special emphasis should be placed on the fact that the voyage was one of discovery, and notice should be taken of the inventions which made such voyage possible.

1.   Other discoveries: a. the Cabots, the claim of England; b. Vespecci, his character vindicated.

IV.   Explorations.

a.   Spanish results: 1, Ponce de Leon; 2, Babao; 3, De Soto,

b.   French results: 1, Verrazani; 2, Cartier; 3, Champlain; 4; Jesuits; 5, Marquette and Joliet; 6, La Salle.

c.   English results: 1, Drake; 2, Raleigh; 3, London Company; 4, Plymoth Company.

d.   Dutch Results: Hudson.

V.   Settlements and colonies.

a.   Virginia: name, John Smith's charter.

b.   Massachusetts: 1, Plymoth Company, settlement, religion; 2, Bay colony, religious troubles, Roger Williams, Quakers.

c.   New Hampshire, early name.

d. Connecticut charter.

e. Rho le Island, religious freedom.

f. New York: Dutch Governors, English Governors.

g. New Jersey.

h. Pennsylvania: William Penn, effect of treaty upon Indians.

i. Delaware: Dutch, Swedes, prohibition of slavery.

j. Maryland: name, Catholics and Protestants.

k. Carolina, Huguenots.

l. Division of Carolina.

m. Georgia: Oglethorpe, characters of settlers.

o. Louisiana, before the purchase from France, French and Spanish governments in Louisiana. The difficulties the colonists had to contend against.

VI. The colonists considered with regard to causes of settlement.

a. Oppression.

VII. The colonists considered with regard to form of government.

a. Charter; *b* Proprietary; *c.* Provincial.

VII. Life and manners in the colonies, dwellings, dress, laws town-meeting, education, employment

IX. Growth of ideas of Independence.

a. Feelings of the colonists under oppression.

b. Increase of privileges.

d. New England confederation.

e. Convention of 1754, Franklin's plan.

X. Revolution.

Reasons for navigation act, taxation, stamp act, etc.

XI. Articles of confederation, purpose, nature, objects.

b Constitutional convention, plans proposed, compromises made, formation of political parties.

XII. Discussion of leading principles of the Constitution.

XIII. Causes of war of 1812. Short sketches of political parties from the formation of the Constitution. "Right of Search." War between England and France. Orders in Council. Milan decree. Embargo Act, etc.

XIV. United States History completed.

XV. Growth and development. Agriculture, commerce, manufacturers, literature, education, etc.

a.—Inventions: Franklin, Whitney, Fulton, Morse, McCormick, George Howe, Edison, Bell.

XVI. Review of wars.

Indian: Virginia, King Phillips, Pequod, Pontiac, Miamis, Creek, Black Hawk, Florida, West and Northwest.

Foreign: King William, Queen Anne, King George, French and Indian, the Revolution, Tripolitan, 1812, Algiers, Mexican.

Civil: Bacon's Rebellion, Clayborne's Rebellion, Whiskey Insurrection, Dow's Rebellion, Mormon.

United States. Completed.

DRAWING AND WRITING.

Copy-book No. 4 and 5. Analysis and free-hand exercises continued. Designs (straight and curve lines) furnished by teacher.
Original designs by pupils.

CONCLUDING REMARKS.

This outline of studies is submitted to the consideration of
teachers and patrons.

The educational reformers affirm that the science of education
is in advance of the art of teaching.

This conclusion is unavoidable after having read Herbert
Spencer and other modern authors, who have given the subject
careful attention.

Should this synopsis give rise to inquiry and discussion, the
outline will not have been uselessly presented.

J. A. B.

www.ingramcontent.com/pod-product-compliance
Lightning Source LLC
Chambersburg PA
CBHW031441280326
41927CB00038B/1401